D♡A♡T♡I♡N♡G
Your Customer®

D♥A♥T♥I♥N♥G *Your Customer*®

A Relationship Manual

James D. Feldman
CSP™, CITE, CPIM, CPC®, CPT®, MIP, PCS

Copyright © 2019 James Feldman

All rights reserved. No part of this book may be reproduced or transmitted in any form or by any means, electronic or mechanical, including photocopying, recording, or by any information storage and retrieval system, without permission in writing from the publisher.

Published by Open Books Press, USA

www.openbookspress.com
info@openbookspress.com

An imprint of Pen & Publish, Inc.
www.PenandPublish.com
Bloomington, Indiana
(314) 827-6567

Print ISBN: 978-1-941799-52-9

Cover Design: Michelle Hove
www.HovePaintingStudio.com

Printed on acid-free paper.

NOTICE

Just like any manual or toolbox, you should carefully consider the risk/rewards of any changes to your Customer Service policies. We all can't manage the behavior of our Customers, employees, or suppliers without a culture change. This manual is based on personal experience, extensive reading, and subjective evidence from some of my clients. Although I have made every reasonable attempt to achieve complete accuracy of the content in this manual, I assume no responsibility for errors or omissions.

This information is offered as a thought starter. Your individual or corporate circumstances might not be exactly suited to the examples illustrated here, so you should adjust your use of the information and recommendations accordingly.

Any trademarks, service marks, product names, or named features are assumed to be the property of their respective owners, and they are used only for reference. No implied endorsement exists if I use one of these terms.

All quotes used in this manual are copyrights of their owners.

Original art created by Michelle Hove | michelleehove@gmail.com

Contents

Foreword by Christine Churchill viii
Preface ix
Who Is Jim Feldman? xii
About this Manual xiv
Five Rapport-Building Tips to Help You DATE Your Customers . . xvii
A "Crash Course" on Customer Service xix
The Objective Is to Get Your Customer to Return xx
Introduction 1
Customer Service Isn't a Department—It's an Attitude 3
D Is for DAZZLE 18
A Is for ANTICIPATE 48
T Is for TREAT 77
I Is for INNOVATION 103
N Is for NURTURE 126
G Is for GUARANTEE 147
AHAs 165
Acknowledgments 178

Foreword

Savvy, educated, digitally social consumers are all around us. This is terrific news for some companies, but most companies live in constant fear of being "found out" or called out on poor service delivery.

It is no longer enough to simply have a customer service team that are available to respond to customers. Customers are seeking enhanced emotional experiences at every turn. Beyond this, customer are "posting-happy" and welcome the opportunity to share a "woe is me" experience on social media.

If I asked you to think of one example where an experience mentioned on social media gravely affected a company, I imagine each of you could think of at least five that have occurred in the last month leading towards catastrophic outcomes for the organization and their team members.

Forever on guard, companies are challenged about where to turn and how best to pro-actively serve their customers and anticipate their needs.

In Jim's newest edition of DATING Your Customer®: A Relationship Manual, customer service and operational leaders will find an exceptional resource that is broken down into easily digestible, actionable, content. This book will act as a guide to navigating the shark-infested waters of delivering exceptional customer experiences.

This book is perfect for all team members as a resource, and for internal training opportunities. The language used, numerous lists, as well as the AHAs section of the book, allow for content to be understandable and easily applied in the context of your specific organization or role.

Congratulations on purchasing this book! Use the information thoughtfully and have fun while learning all the exceptional ways to delight your customers, while also building lifelong relationships.

Christine Churchill
Managing Director, Customer Service Institute of America
Serviceinstitute.com

Preface

No matter what you call them, Customers, Clients, Passengers, Patients, Employees, Suppliers, or Families these are the people who buy and recommend your products or Services. They all use products or Services of someone's organization and they always compare your Service—good or bad—to the Service they get elsewhere.

My vet is more involved with my pets after a visit than my surgeon or primary care doctor is with me. I always compare my vet to my primary care doctor or surgeon. *Too bad,* I often think to myself, *that my vet doesn't work on me.*

No matter what you sell, you want it to be good. You want to exceed their expectations, no matter how high or unreasonable, if you want to keep your Customers. While you may or may not agree with your Customer, you certainly want to keep them.

The premise of this manual is simple: build a good relationship with your Customer.

Just like dating, it's much easier to create a good relationship from the onset than to struggle with a bad one.

"If we are not Customer-driven, our cars won't be either."
—Henry Ford

Successful dates build on one another. If the first one is positive and upbeat, then a second date is often the reward. The same with a Customer.

The first date often shapes the attitude of the Customer and their behavior.

If the first sale makes the Customer feel special, they often return.

This manual was designed as a catalyst for enlightened companies. If you aren't ready to make "shifts" in the way you treat your Customers, Employees, and Suppliers, then this dialogue isn't for you.

FAIR WARNING: This program is going to confront you to change some of your beliefs. I'm going to make you a little uncomfortable. Maybe a lot uncomfortable.

If you're ready to make this happen, congratulations! If not, then at least read with an open mind.

Who knows? Perhaps something I say might help you change some of your thinking.

This is the year to create YOUR year of success.

This isn't someone else's year.

This isn't next year. Or next month. Or tomorrow. This is it. Now. Right now.

I am going to encourage you to change the way you look at your organization.

Shifts are taking place and they offer you either a threat or an opportunity.

Please write down three words as my "Three Rs" for building your Customer relationships.

1. Relate
2. Resonate
3. Reinforce

To create an opportunity for your profession, you have to "shift" your Customer Service policies and make them more valuable to the community of potential Customers than they have ever been before.

In reality, there's only one way to "shift" the conduct of your Customers. This is by shifting your own actions. All you can do to manage the relationship with your Customer is to take the initiative and behave in a positive manner. If you provide remarkable Service, this makes your Customers feel privileged. This means creating "insistence" in the way you obtain and retain your Customers. The easiest way to create this insistence is to create a monogamous relationship. Just like dating, you can play the field for only so long. Once you find a Customer with great potential, then you can get to know what satisfies them. I know you're thinking, "Come on, Jim, one Customer? How can I survive?" It's all about managing the relationship. Instead of taking one Customer for granted, if you think of that Customer as your ONLY Customer, and demonstrate it by making them feel important, they'll normally reciprocate.

According to Jim:
Make your Customer feel important.
Shift Happens!® when you do.

In case you aren't familiar with the term "Shift Happens!®" it refers to shifts in thinking, actions, or results that are part of any kind of change. Two kinds of "shift" usually hit the fan: those for which we have no control and those we can make an effort to change.

I wrote this manual to provide you with a view that ultimately proves to be so compelling, you can never see a thing in quite the same way again. I gathered insights and examples that might make you uncomfortable, challenge your assumptions, and force you to revisit how you D-A-T-E your Customers.

Success isn't about incremental improvements.

Success is about bold, fundamental differences that create insistence.

According to Jim:
Salespersons are promise makers.
  Customer Service persons are promise keepers.

Don't forget to ask for the sale.

Who Is Jim Feldman?

Jim Feldman is provocative, controversial, and outside conventional wisdom. He thinks "inside the box" to obtain the core issues of ineffective Customer Service and return policies. **Jim provides plain talk for smart people.** The author of over a dozen books, and hundreds of articles and speeches, Jim has been a sought-after consultant to many Fortune 500 companies.

Jim offers uncommon common-sense explanations for complex issues. He moves past pop management rhetoric to focus on the central truths that lead to success. He provides practical information you can apply immediately. Jim believes his job isn't complete unless his readers are challenged to take specific action.

For over four decades, Jim has been challenging businesses to unleash personal and organizational creativity, uniqueness, and innovation, while revealing the essential innovative skills needed to achieve unconventional policies and inventive results. His goal is to delight Customers and to develop new resources for growth, profits, and competitive advantage. Jim's vision is to create great Customer Experiences that develop Customer Insistence. Customers have many choices. It's all about bringing your Customers back . . . not sending them away.

Jim has been a board member for over a dozen associations and a seventy-story high rise. He holds every certification his industry offers and is a visiting professor at Roosevelt University. Jim has written fourteen books—seven on Customer Service—over 400 articles, and he's been a keynote business speaker presenting for such diverse organizations as the US Department of Defense, Verizon, Toyota, Kodak, March of Dimes, Hewlett-Packard, Apple Computer, and the Cremation Association of North America, to name only a few.

Jim helped create Customer Experiences for both start-ups and Fortune 500 companies. He understands that organizations must create a foundation of Customer-focused survival philosophies that have one goal: get the Customer to return. Jim's clients include Toyota, Apple, Neutrogena, Coca-Cola, Microsoft, Helene Curtis, ECMC, Mary Kay, Creative Memories, The Pampered Chef, Lexus, Xerox, MGM Resorts and Casinos, Wynn Las Vegas, Department of Defense, Verizon, Foxwoods Resort and Casino, Hewlett-Packard, Vidal Sassoon, and more.

After attending law school, Jim was accepted as the first applicant for the University of Illinois (U of I) Executive MBA program. Upon completion of the program, Jim became a visiting professor at U of I, Roosevelt University, Purdue University, Northeastern Illinois University, and Kendall College.

Jim's educational background and business experience allow him to work with people at any level, as well as with companies of all sizes.

He is a consultant to businesses, associations, veterans, and entire communities.

Jim is also a serial entrepreneur who owns several businesses that provide ongoing insights into Customer Service, problem solving, team building, and leadership.

Jim is actively involved in several trade associations, as well as previously being a member of their Board of Directors.

A frequent contributor to charitable organizations, as well as for-profits, Jim's insights are learned first-hand—in the trenches—with real-world opportunities and challenges. Jim was a board or trustee member of the

- Direct Selling Association
- Incentive Research Federation
- Association of Incentive Marketing
- University of Chicago Cancer Research Board
- Y-ME Breast Cancer Organization
- National Premium Sales Executive
- Society for Incentive Travel Excellence

He was also on the advisory board for A Safe Haven, and Pets Are Worth Saving. Jim understands that not-for-profit is a tax status not a business model. The same holds true for companies that believe their Customers aren't appreciating assets.

According to Jim:

Never confuse inconvenient with impossible.

About this manual...

This manual can be used by anyone interested in learning more about Customer Service or starting a discussion about how to improve Customer Service in your department. It provides tools to help people become more aware of the issues and how to move forward on those issues. The goal of this manual is twofold: first, to give the Customer Service Team the tools and power to raise awareness about Customer Service and, second, to empower the team to think about the actions to influence both policies and systems to address issues more effectively.

You should find this manual stimulating, idea-generating, provocative, and unique. If you agree with 100 percent of what I offer, I've failed because that's what you expected when you bought this manual. Your expectations and thoughts for making this purchase are no different from any other Customer. You didn't have to buy this manual. You had many choices. You chose this manual because you're interested in getting—and keeping—more Customers. What took place is similar to dating. An offer was made. Expectations were created. And, together, we consummated our experience. Just like dating, to keep you as a Customer (or a date), it's necessary to continue paying attention to your expectations. Today's Customers are more demanding. They want a quality product or Service—faster and cheaper.

This manual uses the terms of D-A-T-I-N-G to clarify how to do something you already know and to provide you with the tools you need. It seems like such a simple idea—great Service makes for loyal Customers and more profits. Great dates lead to marriage and a life together. But, apparently, it isn't so simple because many of the companies that want to do business with us have decided great Service isn't worth the cost. The goals of dating are the same as D-A-T-I-N-G: you must decide to exceed expectations to retain the relationship.

You'll also find words other than Dazzle, Anticipate, Treat, Nurture, Innovate, and Guarantee in each section of D-A-T-I-N-G. These words are intended to broaden your understanding of how different companies look at their Customer Service needs or wants.

This is a manual full of exciting tools and easy-to-grasp concepts. Dealing with Customers and clients requires working with human beings, not things. As a result, you must function with personalities, tempers, moods, expectations, and, sometimes, misunderstandings. Each person feels unique, special, and different. Customer Service is a dynamic, not a static, operation. Customers measure the qualify of an organization by the quality of the Customer Service provided.

Nordstrom has legendary Customer Service. Its competition might sell an identical product for less, but Nordstrom's innovative approach allows them to find out what the Customer values and deliver it to them. The stories are legendary because Nordstrom has built its business on one-to-one communication. Costco and Zappos are two companies that also strive to deliver exceptional Customer Service with a lower price than many of their competitors: that's "the perfect storm." When great Service is joined by great prices, competition is forced to compete in a new world of price and value.

Throughout this book, you can find examples you can apply to your business or Service. It's all about building relationships with your Customers, employees, and suppliers to create AHA! moments. There's a lot of psychological work in keeping everyone happy. Maybe you didn't plan this, but you have one of the most difficult jobs on the planet. It's heavy-duty work that doesn't get the amount of attention, dedication, and recognition it deserves. This manual is about creating some of those AHA!s that can be shared, replicated, and deposited into your "relationship capital" account. It will earn interest.

Use this manual as a thought-starter to find those AHA! moments. Once you hear the AHA! in your head, you've found that focused, singular "tool" to add to your toolbox.

About the wide margins . . .

The wide outside margins are lined so you can take notes. The margins are yours to customize this manual to your wants, needs, and values. The more you write in the margins, the more value this manual has for you. It's your manual. Make it work for you. When you find my AHA!, use a highlighter to ensure you can find your own AHA! The more notes you take—and implement—the greater your influence to ensure that Shift Happens!®

About Customer Service . . .

If you realize Customer Service isn't your top priority, you're losing Customers. And, if you don't address Customers as a top priority ASAP, your Customers will soon find someone who *will* treat them as a VIP. The purpose of this manual is to help you realize Customers are the reason you have a business. Without Customers, no matter what you do, there isn't any business.

Most companies have many products and Customers with different wants, needs, values, and expectations. You can't know everything about everything.

According to Jim:
Don't let what you think you know stop you from learning what you need to know.

US Businesses Annually Lose An Estimated $93 BILLION Due to Poor Customer Service

Five Rapport-Building Tips to Help You DATE Your Customers

Sometimes, when you read a book or manual, you discover you really want to learn the basic information it contains. When you read this manual, open your mind to new ideas and suggestions that could make it easier for you to do business.

According to Jim:
Nothing changes if nothing changes.

Customers have choices. Customers vote with their money. If they spend money with you, then they have made a decision based on what you offer, what you promise, and what you deliver.

Just like dating, you have only one chance to make a first impression. That impression requires some modification for each occurrence. One Size Does Not Fit All. Whether it's learning how to find your soul mate or the perfect product, each of us goes through an evaluation process. To become desirable, use these five tips to help you succeed.

1) Establish a Common Ground

Your Customers relate to people who are most like themselves. They want to feel a connection with you beyond just being a client. This means you need to quickly establish a common ground with each Customer.

2) Listen and Show Concern

Your Customer always wants to talk about their most favorite topic: themselves and their situation, wants, or needs. The more you talk about yourself or your business, the more you turn your Customer away. In general, people don't take an active interest in a stranger's life. This means you need to stand out by building a relationship—talk about your Customer and offer compliments, when appropriate. Listening involves so much more than simply not talking. Listening is a matter of understanding your Customer. Give your Customer your full attention and make them feel important.

3) Use Humor

One of the quickest ways to build rapport is through humor. A good joke or a funny story eases tension and helps to break down mental barriers. It also shows your Customers your softer, more human side.

4) Keep a Positive Attitude

When you're positive and upbeat, people naturally want to be around you and do business with you. Unfortunately, in today's world, seeds of negativity are all around us, from traffic jams to 50+ hour workweeks. But how we choose to look at those situations determines not only our own mood, but also our Customer's mood.

When you look at any situation in a positive light, everything around you also becomes positive. Then your mindset shifts from negative to positive, which, in turn, "tricks" your body into feeling more alert, more alive, and more free. And, even more important, your positive attitude rubs off on others, creating a more harmonious environment for your Customers.

5) Treat Customers Like Family

Your Customers want to know that you have their best interests at heart. They want to sense a "we're in this together" attitude. You can easily accomplish this by being genuinely happy and excited to talk with them.

This manual is about creating a culture that encourages motivated men and women—just like you—to acquire the entrepreneurial mindset of an owner. Your goal should be to make the extra effort necessary to develop and deliver Customer Service that exceeds your Customers' expectations.

According to Jim:

D ۰ A ۰ T ۰ I ۰ N ۰ G Your Customer® has one objective: to guarantee that you continue to have Customers in the future.

James Feldman

A "Crash Course" on Customer Service

The 10th most important words:
"I apologize for our mistake. Let me make it right"

The 9th most important words:
"Thank you for your business. Please come back again."

The 8th most important words:
"I'm not sure, but I will find out."

The 7th most important words:
"What else can I do for you?"

The 6th most important words:
"What is most convenient for you?"

The 5th most important words:
"How may I serve you?"

The 4th most important words:
"How did we do?"

The 3rd most important words:
"I'm glad you're here!"

The 2nd most important words:
"Thank you."

The 1st and *most* important word:
"Yes."

According to Jim:

The Customer is still King and they know it. Think of your main task as bringing the Customer back.

The Objective Is to Get Your Customer to Return

Think your Customers are satisfied? They very well may be. But, unfortunately, Customer Satisfaction doesn't always lead to Customer Loyalty. These days, even if your Customers are completely satisfied with your product or Service, 40 percent of them will leave you and start doing business with your competition.

On the surface, 40 percent might not seem like that much. After all, over half your satisfied Customers are coming back. But, in dollars and cents, 40 percent is costing you more than you might think. According to the *Wall Street Journal,* attracting new Customers can cost nearly double the amount it takes to attract repeat business from your existing Customer base.

What's the solution? Quite simply, to retain all your Customers and increase your sales, you need to go beyond Customer Satisfaction and develop the rapport that makes your Customers adore you. Only then can you achieve true Customer Loyalty.

The good news is this: developing exceptional Customer rapport is easier than you may think. It's just like dating. In the past, the challenges of dating were very different. Men and women wanted a partner, someone to share their life, someone to share a feeling of security, and someone they could share a family with.

We all seem to want someone who supports us on most levels—emotional, spiritual, social, mental, financial, and physical—but not necessarily family development. It's no longer enough to find someone to marry us; we want partners in every sense, in every part of our life.

This change has required us to update our dating skills, to refine who we are, and to improve how we communicate with others. It has become more of a skill. Our potential partner is now more interested in the entire package, rather than only one major area of focus, such as physical attraction. We want it all. It's the same in attempting to obtain Customers and exceeding their expectations. Customer Service is demanding. Organizations are going to shrink, consolidate, and close unless someone does what you do—satisfy the needs and wants of your Customers.

According to Jim:

Live in the FUTURE.
  Appreciate WISDOM.
  FORGET permanence.
  Change your FOCUS.
  Get excited and accept RISK.
  FOCUS on your Customer and
  the money will follow.

When you go beyond Customer Satisfaction and create true Customer Loyalty, you develop a long-term relationship, which leads to increased profits. The end result is having Customers who love you, as well as a business that grows and thrives. When this happens, Customers insist on doing business with you. Creating Customer Insistence should be the goal of every company that wants to succeed and grow.

Each letter in D-A-T-I-N-G stands for a word or action that helps you create Customer Insistence. And, just like dating, the objective is to get the second date.

Now, don't get me wrong. Dating and Customer Service are similar, but they're definitely not the same. Dates often lead to physical relationships, marriage, and children, but D-A-T-I-N-G leads to repeat business and referrals.

I chose one word for each letter to describe the process, but I also offer other suggestions. Find the words that work best for you and your organization, and then create your own D-A-T-I-N-G rapport-building. As you read this manual, make notes to yourself that help reinforce the principles of great Service.

An old joke tells about two guys walking in the woods when a bear starts to chase them. Later that day, one of the guys is in a bar retelling the story. One listener asks, "How did you out run the bear?" "I didn't have to," was the reply. "I only had to out run the other guy." Customer Service excellence is similar. It was never that you had to be so great, it was just that everyone else is so bad.

My 2018 list for the worst Customer Service:

1. Comcast Business: Internet, cable television & telephone provider
2. Citibank Mortgage: residential mortgage
3. LunarPages: website hosting service
4. Comcast Residential: Internet, cable television & telephone provider
5. USPS: Chicago mail delivery

My 2018 list for the best Customer Service:

1. Zappos & Zenni Optical (tied)
2. Nordstrom: retailer that replicates great Service at 116 stores in the US. While it was previously at #1, Nordstrom Rack continues to pull down the CS rating I have for Nordstrom. Too bad when the 'rack' prices are discounted, the service is also discounted.
3. ABT: retail appliances & electronics (one location outside Chicago)
4. Amazon
5. JetBlue Airlines

Assignment

Before you read any further in this manual, please make your own worst and best Customer Service list. Then keep sidebar notes about why the companies are on one list or the other. Think about how each company could migrate from one list to the other. What would it take to move the worst companies to the best list, and vice versa?

What follows is my D-A-T-I-N-G Your Customer® Manual. Use it well.

According to Jim:
Don't fear change. Embrace it enthusiastically. Encourage and drive it.

James Feldman

Introduction

As a marketer, I'm horrified and disenchanted by the way you and I are treated as Customers. I'm confident we would agree that different companies find themselves polarized by the price differential. But why would those same companies position themselves on one end as providing exceptional Service and ignoring Customer Service issues altogether on the other end? What's more amazing is that all of them—good and bad—say they provide great Customer Service.

What might be a major factor is that many businesses don't consider themselves in the Service business. Regardless of your industry, profession, Service, or product, you must remember you actually are in the Service business. Let's be honest. In the last few years, most products that weren't well made followed the dodo bird into extinction. Companies that claimed great Service, but delivered marginal products, moved into those vacated positions. Then, almost every surviving company found that product differentiation was really exceptional Customer Service. New companies that focused on great Service displaced those that were marginal. In 1999, one of those new companies was a shoe company called Zappos.

Make the Traditionalists Squirm

Data from Internet Retailer shows that online retail sales in the US jumped 15 percent from 2017 to 2018 to pass $517 billion. Conversely, physical stores only saw a growth of 3.7 percent. After factoring out items not normally purchased online, such as fuel and automobiles, e-commerce now accounts for 14.3 percent of total retail sales. In just a decade, the web has more than doubled its share of retail sales.

The Zappos vision:

"People will buy from the company with the best Service and the best selection. Zappos.com will be that online store."

Hsieh likes to tell the story of Roger Bannister's inspirational four-minute mile, and how that feat seemed like an impossible accomplishment. Then, after Bannister became the first to break the four-minute mark in 1954, another man, Australia's John Landy, ran another sub-four-minute mile. "It wasn't like nutrition suddenly improved," Hsieh said. "It was that people suddenly believed it could be done."

"A great brand," Hsieh said, "is a story that never stops unfolding."

"We decided to be about providing the best Service. We said, 'We're a Service company that just happens to sell shoes.' We interview people for culture fit. We want people who are passionate about what Zappos is about—Service. At Zappos, we want people to call us. We believe that forming personal, emotional connections with our Customers is the best way to provide great Service."

—Tony Hsieh, CEO, zappos.com

According to Jim:

D A T I N G Your Customers® is all about ATTITUDE, which determines your altitude. Listen more than you talk. ACT delighted.

Customer Service Isn't a Department— It's an Attitude

Nearly every business claims their Customer Service is a big reason to do business with them. Yet, from the Customer's perspective, good Service is what they expect to receive when they make a purchase in any industry or profession. If you learn the six principles in D-A-T-I-N-G, your objective shouldn't be just to have satisfied Customers, but to have delighted advocates for your enterprise. If you still aren't convinced, look at the hard evidence of Zappos. For years, people have paid lip service to the importance of great Customer Service. Bain & Company did a study to place a dollar amount on the impact of Customer Service on the bottom line. They learned that a 5 percent increase in Customer Retention can increase profits as much as from 25 percent to 100 percent, depending on the industry. See the following chart.

Increase in retention	Industry	Results
5%	Insurance	+ 60% profits
4%	Employer Services (payroll, etc.)	+ 21% profits
5%	Banking	+ 40% profits
5%	Laundry	+ 60% profits

—Bain & Company

The previous situation takes place for two reasons:

1. It costs five times more to get a new Customer than it does to retain an existing one.
2. When you offer personalized, relevant, and timely Customer Service, you create a differentiation that creates what I call "Customer Insistence."

Commoditization has become rampant in most industries. As you know, commoditization occurs when attributes such as product specs, price, availability, Service, and brand are given economic value. This occurs as a result of the constant messaging from nearly every enterprise about their products, platform, and processes and Service.

Somehow, despite all the Customer Service degradation, sales are made, marketing continues, and commerce grows. Shift happened because we no longer buy from vendors to whom we're loyal. We buy from vendors where we find the least amount of hassle, the least apathy, and the least arrogance. We have learned to accept mediocrity and to gravitate to the lowest level of mediocrity we can accept. That's how Shift Happens!®

What's required is to build a moat around your Customers and focus on—and to consistently deliver—an elevated experience in all your interactions. In preparation for this manual, I interviewed many salespeople, administrators, and Customers. During my first visit to a Nordstrom's in southern California, I met a salesman in the men's department. He greeted me with a question: "Did you come in for the dress shirt sale?" That started a dialogue, which not only resulted in a sales for him, but also in a follow-up that delivered a product I was looking for, which wasn't available in his store location.

I now recant this experience in every one of my Customer Service presentations. I say, "This salesman should have charged admission. Dealing with him was a show, not unlike watching a well-trained sports team or a symphony conductor. He knew every move, every objection, and every solution. Each time I recall this event, the salesman's stature grows because he had the ability to make me feel as though I were his only Customer."

As I checked out, the salesman asked me if I were looking for anything else in the store. I said I was looking for the Limited Edition Trafalar braces (suspenders to those of you who think suspenders and braces are the same thing, which they aren't) that depicted the Statue of Liberty, fireworks, etc. He took out a small card and made a note. Three weeks later, a package from Anchorage, Alaska, arrived with the sought-after braces.

The note inside read, "Dear Mr. Feldman, I believe these are the braces you are looking for. If you want to keep them, we will charge the credit card you used at our South Coast Plaza store. If not, please return them using the supplied UPS label and call tag. Nicole, your personal shopper."

It was my AHA! Customer Service moment.

According to Jim:

If you stop worrying about money and concentrate on providing great Customer Service, the money will follow.

Now, it's time to start D-A-T-I-N-G Your Customer®

Approach Customer Service the same way you approach a date. It's about building a relationship. Nurture it with good habits and constant Service. Each date builds on the previous one. Each sale does the same in building Customer Retention. Remember, your Customer is always right—sometimes they're confused, misinformed, rude, stubborn, or changeable—but they're never wrong. Ever date anyone like that? In addition, make sure every time you refer to the word "Customer," it's capitalized. This is simply one more way to alert everyone to the Customer importance. Use their name whenever possible. Refer to them by name on the phone, online, in email, and in snail mail. Remember, without paying Customers, no one has a job.

"It's not creative unless it sells."

—David Olgivy, advertising legend

You PROVIDE solutions...
not deliver products.
You CREATE value...
not provide services.
You ENGAGE your Customers
not sell to them.
You are PROBLEM SOLVERS...
who charge for your WISDOM.

Everyone might not agree with Harry Gordon Selfridge's oft quoted "The Customer is always right," but it is certainly never a good practice to simply assume that a Customer is wrong.

In March 2017, United Airlines CEO Oscar Munoz was named US Communicator of the Year by the magazine *PRWeek.* Just one month later, his company's poor response to a Customer incident turned into a PR disaster, caused its stock to dramatically drop one billion dollars in value, and has placed the entire airline industry under the microscope. Here's a look at how the situation escalated, explaining how, through the power of social media, an isolated incident turned into a global PR disaster overnight.

United Airlines suffered the mother of all social media crises when a video of law enforcement officers dragging a passenger forcibly off one of its planes went viral.

April 9, 2017

Security officials dragged paying passenger Dr. David Dao off United Express Flight 3411 from Chicago to Louisville, Kentucky. As a result of his rough treatment, Dr. Dao was hospitalized.

April 10, 2017

Outrage explodes on social media after a video emerged of Dr. Dao being violently removed from United Airlines Flight 3411 bound for Louisville. Four Chicago Department of Aviation security officers rip the passenger out of his seat, bloodying him in the process.

Dr. David Dao was a 69-year-old Vietnamese American doctor from Elizabethtown, Kentucky. When asked to give up his seat for United employees after Flight 3411 was overbooked, he refused. He paid for the seat. He was already seated. Can you imagine what other passengers were thinking? Do you see the problem?

Companies, governments, etc., make mistakes all the time; whether they experience a PR disaster depends on how they respond.

United Airlines CEO Oscar Munoz's response amplified the incident.

The first official response from United Airlines CEO should have offered an unreserved apology to Dr. Dao and his wife after he was forcibly removed from his seat and dragged down the aircraft aisle. Instead, Oscar Munoz failed to acknowledge the injuries Dr. Dao suffered, apologizing only for having to "re-accommodate Customers."

> "This is an upsetting event to all of us here at United. I apologize for having to re-accommodate these customers. Our team is moving with a sense of urgency to work with the authorities and conduct our own detailed review of what happened. We are also reaching out to this passenger to talk directly to him and further address and resolve this situation."
>
> —Oscar Munoz, CEO, United Airlines

On top of this unsympathetic response, a leaked internal email from Munoz to United Airlines staff described the passenger as "disruptive and belligerent" and that "employees followed established procedures for dealing with situations like this."

This lack of empathy in United Airlines response added fuel to the fire and caused another wave of backlash toward the company on social media. Who advised Munoz? What were they thinking?

April 12, 2017

Details about Dr. Dao's past begin to circulate through the media, but the court of public opinion still rules against United.

Munoz appears on *Good Morning America* to issue another apology, saying the video made him feel ashamed.

Calls for a boycott mount as observers in China, where United derives two billion dollars in revenue, and elsewhere speculate the Flight 3411 incident was racially motivated.

April 13, 2017

Tom Demetrio, a Chicago-based attorney representing Dr. Dao, holds a press conference and denounces United for treating passengers like "cattle." Demetrio explains Dr. Dao suffered a concussion, a broken nose, injury to the sinuses, and the loss of two front teeth during the incident. His client will undergo reconstructive surgery shortly.

United reiterates its apologies, saying it will never use law enforcement to remove passengers "unless it's a matter of safety and security."

United Master Executive Council, the union representing the airline's 12,500 pilots, releases a statement expressing their anger. The statement also says it had nothing to do with the incident.

April 16, 2017

United confirms media reports it has changed it overbooking policy. Now, crew members can't remove passengers who are already seated.

April 19, 2017

Munoz meets with the Chinese consulate in Chicago "over the possible impact to bookings" as social media users across the US, China, and Vietnam call for a boycott of United.

April 22, 2017

Two separate surveys by Morning Consult and LendEdu reach similar findings that more than 40% of millennials would either no longer fly on United or avoid giving it their business.

Munoz exacerbated an already fraught situation with a robotic response and barely concealed contempt for his Customers.

In a highly competitive price-led industry dominated by a few players, United failed to show empathy with its paying Customers and came across as uncaring, insincere, and brutal.

April 25, 2017

Munoz apologized for the forcible removal of Dr. Dao, calling the incident "truly horrific" and offered his "deepest apologies."

Munoz also said in the statement, "I want you to know that we take full responsibility and we will work to make it right; I promise you we will do better."

By the time the second official response from the CEO was released, United was still struggling to contain the fallout from the incident. Social media was trending with users tweeting memes and slogans such as "not enough seating, prepare for a beating."

United Airlines should have moved much more quickly to limit damage from the video. **This fiasco demonstrates the importance of a company's first response and how it is delivered.**

United underestimated the power of social media.

This incident highlights the power of social media, and how one isolated incident can become a global PR disaster overnight. The days of a company getting away with such incidents are gone due to smartphones, and any incident has the potential to be seen by millions, something companies need to be aware of.

Multiple passengers on Flight 3411 were able to record and post the event in real time for the world to see; before the plane touched down in Louisville, the incident had been viewed by people all over the world.

Additionally, once shared on social media, companies like United Airlines have no control or ability to take photos or videos down.

One moment of bad Customer service and the whole airline industry is under a microscope.

The practice of "bumping" on an aircraft is common practice among all airlines and is a key part of how the industry runs. There are always people who are late for a flight and therefore to ensure there are minimal empty seats, airlines often overbook flights. If there are more passengers than available seats, the airline offers flight credit in exchange for being inconvenienced to take the next flight.

In the case of Flight 3411, United needed to "bump" four passengers to get four crew members to Louisville to fly a crewless plane. Inconveniencing four passengers on one flight is better than cancelling a flight and inconveniencing over two hundred passengers. United offered the four passengers (one of which was Dr. Dao) $1,000 in flight credit—airline staff could have offered up to $1,300 but chose not to. Dr. Dao refused to give up his seat and instead of bumping another passenger, Dr. Dao was forcibly removed from the aircraft. In retrospect the bad decisions cost United millions if not billions of dollars. Heads up! After this incident, Customers now know that if they wait longer, the airline will offer more money to bump them.

May 2017

Things continue to get worse for United Airlines: one month after the incident, a giant rabbit died on United Airlines flight from London to Chicago. An incident like this would not normally make international news, but because of their previous mistakes, the entire world was scrutinizing every move United Airlines was making.

May 22, 2017

Despite the current blunders, Munoz led the airline industry in 2016 in total compensation.

Per United's filings with the US Securities and Exchange Commission, Munoz earned a whopping $18.7 million in 2016. In addition to a $1.2 million salary, he earned incentives and a signon bonus from 2015.

While the board determined that United met its goals in metrics such as on-time arrival, pre-tax income, and return on invested capital, Munoz's targets were changed in 2017, "with the board recently announcing executive compensation will be more closely tied to United's customer service metrics. The decision, made public after United's recent debacle in Chicago in which security officers forcibly removed a passenger, is designed to promote, 'necessary cultural and process change,' the board said."

With these CEOs earning millions, don't you think they would focus on the passenger experience more closely? While Munoz was paid the most in 2016, his airline is at the bottom of the CS Score. Brad Tilden's salary is 1/6 of Munoz's; Alaska Airlines has the highest rating. Go figure?

COMPARING 2016 AIRLINE CEO COMPENSATION WITH PRIOR YEARS

CEO	Airline	2014 Pay	2015 Pay	2016 Pay
Oscar Munoz *	United Airlines	N/A	$5,795,459	$18,720,548
Ed Bastian **	Delta Air Lines	$9,009,330	$9,046,574	$12,557,231
Doug Parker	American Airlines	$12,301,976	$11,418,547	$11,140,763
Bob Fornaro ***	Spirit Airlines	N/A	N/A	$7,172,512
Gary Kelly	Southwest Airlines	$5,002,785	$5,947,505	$6,181,660
Brad Tilden	Alaska Airlines	$3,468,722	$3,602,889	$4,246,312
Mark Dunkerley	Hawaiian Airlines	$3,103,945	$3,275,327	$3,731,714
Maury Gallagher	Allegiant Air	$1,078,218	$3,550,486	$3,571,205
Robin Hayes ****	JetBlue Airways	$1,876,898	$3,276,159	$3,160,901

* Munoz became United's CEO in September 2015.
** Bastian became Delta's CEO in May 2016. Earlier pay was from his stint as president.
*** Fornaro joined Spirit as CEO in January 2016.
*** Hayes became JetBlue's CEO in February 2016 after serving as the airline's president.

Note: Data comes from airline filings and a recent report from Joseph W. DeNardi, an analyst with Stifel, with comments from Skift reporter Brian Sumers.

D-A-T-I-N-G YOUR CUSTOMER management tips

- ♥ Respond quickly to Customer incidents, apologizing directly to the impacted people with empathy.
- ♥ Get the facts straight, so that as a company you are fully aware of every detail of the situation.
- ♥ Be transparent with the media. The word "re-accommodate" is forever lodged in the internet lexicon as a United Airlines euphemism for brutally assaulting your Customers.
- ♥ Saying sorry shouldn't be so hard. A good apology only needs to be said once. Then it needs to be followed up with action to demonstrate good intent.

♥ Own your response. If the company made a mistake, own it, apologize for it, and put in place the necessary procedures so it does not happen again.

Observation: Munoz was led too much by legal and internal HR issues that caused him to miss the window of opportunity to make a strong, earnest apology, and his response wasn't consistent with United's stated mission and values.

And other airlines did not learn.

October 2018

Frontier Airlines provided us with a brilliant case study on the importance of Customer experience. It's a great example of how one simple Customer service failure can have serious consequences in the form of a social media maelstrom.

Storms caused Flight 1756 from Des Moines to Orlando to be diverted to Atlanta on July 22, 2018. On the flight were two children, aged seven and nine, returning from a visit to their grandparents.

These kinds of situations, of course, aren't uncommon, and the Frontier staff ensured the children were safe and accompanied by a supervisor at all times. From a safety perspective, Frontier did okay. From a Customer service perspective, however, they failed miserably.

The parents, anxiously waiting for their children, never received any status updates. In fact, the only way they knew the flight was being diverted was through an app they had on their phone.

The Frontier people in Orlando were no help. Had one of their children not borrowed another child's cell phone to briefly text them after landing, they wouldn't have had any information at all. Needless to say, the parents were not happy.

To make matters worse, when Frontier was asked about the incident, the airline's statement was unapologetic, stating that they had just followed standard protocol: "We understand how an unexpected delay caused by weather can be stressful for a parent and our goal is to help passengers get to their destinations as quickly and safely as possible."

I find that Frontier has the worst Customer Experience of any airline, based on my personal accumulation of more than six million miles of flights.

Frontier missed a giant opportunity.

Customer service is, at its foundation, about sending the clear message to Customers that the company cares. It's all about communications, and that is where Frontier, liked United, failed. Imagine how different the outcome would have been had these three simple things happened:

1. A phone call to the parents from Frontier (a human, not a machine), advising them of what is happening, what the next steps will be, and that they will be notified as soon as the plane has landed.

2. A phone call upon landing from the person in charge of supervising the children. The parents would get an update and a phone number they could call if they wanted to check in. They could speak with their children for a few minutes.

3. A phone call as they were leaving for their flight, to confirm that everyone was okay and on their way.

4. Imagine if they got a fourth call a few days later from a concerned Frontier manager just checking in to make sure everything was okay.

Imagine if Frontier had taken the time to make three to four calls to these parents.

The things the parents would say about the airline would be very different indeed. They would be glowing. The reviews would be fantastic. There's a very real chance that it could have been a social media success story. Three little calls.

Southwest Airlines kicks father & toddler off a plane.

A young toddler was sitting on her father's lap prior to takeoff on a Southwest Flight from Chicago to Atlanta. She was crying. Flight attendants had come over to warn the father that she needed to be properly seated, and he was able to settle the young girl—but apparently it wasn't good enough. They were both sitting their seats quietly when the attendants returned to ask them to leave the plane.

It seemed like an extreme measure, but clearly not to the flight attendants who got defensive when other passengers spoke up in the father's defense. One passenger who had observed the initial interaction explained to them that the man had simply asked for a few moments to settle his daughter down, which he did. The attendant's response to this was, "This is not helpful. Do you want to go to Atlanta?" Seriously. She said that.

Working in an airplane cabin is a tremendously challenging position, requiring above-average Customer service skills and legendary patience.

D-A-T-I-N-G Your Customer requires problem-solving skills and the ability to quickly and accurately assess situations—something that wasn't apparent in this situation.

It's either WOW or WHOA. No middle ground.

A 2016 study conducted by The Belding Group, "The Science of 'WOW,'" identified that 71.5 percent of "wow" experiences are negative situations turned around into positive ones. Frontier had one of those opportunities right in front of them—one that could have been turned around with three simple phone calls.

It's a lesson for every organization that is D-A-T-I-N-G Your Customers.

Creating outstanding Customer experiences means sending every Customer the message that the company genuinely cares. Not just cares about their wallets, but about the Customers. It has to come across in every person's action, every process, every policy, and every business practice. Here are three things every company needs:

1. Customer service training and service recovery training for every employee. It's an investment that pays back almost immediately. Avoid e-learning. Get the good stuff.
2. Become one of your own Customers. Look at your business as a Customer. Talk with your Customers. Listen. Examine all your processes, policies, and practices to make sure you are easy to do business with.
3. Care about your Customers, not just their wallets. People are, ultimately, loyal to people. Make sure your team has a Customer-focused attitude and the empowerment to make Customer-focused decisions.

There are still some companies that do a better job, overall, than others.

For example, with Amazon, I have had fantastic experiences with standard issues and questions, but overwhelming frustration with anything that fell in the cracks between their departments or processes. Amazon requires a billion clicks and continual attempts to drive self-serve solutions, then you may eventually get a human as long as you have a standard issue. If you have a non-standard issue, it's good to have a stiff drink handy.

Wayfair has a phone number right on their home page—with humans who are empowered to help. Walmart takes three clicks, but you get the same thing. Nordstrom? Call the store not their HQ or hotline. A real person answers. A real person takes ownership. And you will get a response.

All this to say that I'm not sure if all companies have gone downhill, as much as the hill behind them has grown much bigger and social media piles it on.

It's not getting better. Here's a few examples from 2018 failures at D-A-T-I-N-G:

2018 was a year of unpleasant extremes in Customer interactions. Customer and employee behavior certainly seemed to be significantly different than other years. Many of the stories I saw involved violence on the part of both Customers and employees. We hope it's not a trend.

Cruise ships are not immune to similar issues.

Outstanding Customer service is the hallmark of cruising. A 15-day vacation on a cruise ship is supposed to be a wonderful thing. Norwegian Cruise Lines, however, appears to have forgotten this. No sooner did they leave the port in Miami than passengers began noticing that things weren't quite right. Instead of a tranquil trip, passengers were treated with the sounds of . . . maintenance. The sounds of hammers and grinders were omnipresent. Dust filled the air as decks were sanded down—so much that several passengers had to visit the infirmary with respiratory problems.

It was so bad that close to five hundred angry passengers organized a meeting. They confronted the captain, whose response was to walk out. Norwegian's response after the event was not much better. One has to wonder how if any of the passengers will ever choose Norwegian again.

Amazon Customer service is in the toilet.

Imagine that you've ordered three cartons of toilet paper from Amazon for $88.77. Then imagine that you are charged $7,455 for the shipping costs. Eek. That's what happened to Barbara Carroll in May 2018.

At first, Ms. Carroll wasn't too concerned. Amazon, after all, has a reputation for looking after its Customers. Not this time. She complained to Amazon six times. She wrote a letter to CEO Jeff Bezos. After every complaint, she received a form letter explaining that there would be no refund because the delivery was made on-time and undamaged. Double-yikes—again.

It wasn't until she took the matter to a local television station and the story went viral for Amazon to take action. Two-and-a-half months later, she was finally reimbursed.

Mistakes happen. We all get that. But the unwillingness of Amazon to take ownership over the issue was completely unacceptable.

Poor performance from a performance shop

When Vince Hanson went to pick up his Audi A4 from Titan Motorsports in Orlando in November 2018, the technician took it for one last, very expensive test-drive. He made an illegal U-turn, crashing into another car. No worries—they'll fix it, right? Wrong.

Rather than accept responsibility and offering to fix the damage, the shop told him that the contract he had signed absolved them of any responsibility. They said he would have to go through his own insurance—except the body shop has refused to cooperate with the insurance company. Needless to say, this has led to an ongoing legal battle.

UNHAPPY MEALS

Tom and Tina Olszewski went through a McDonald's drive-thru with their nine-year-old son. After waiting 15 minutes for their order, Tom finally gave up and asked for a refund. The worker refused, then the manager stepped in.

Caught on video is the manager yelling, "Make your own cheeseburger! Teach your son how to cook a f—— hamburger," to the family. One would think that this type of behavior might be close to the top of the "things not to do list" in the McDonald's Customer service training handbook.

A second McDonald's failure to deliver hit social media. A drive-through employee in Cross City, Florida, forgot to turn her headset off as a Customer sat waiting to give his order. He listened to her ranting to another employee for about 45 seconds, then began to record her. The result was more ranting, complaining about the Customer showing up, and describing a failed drug deal.

The mistake, of course, was not really that she forgot about the microphone. It was that she didn't care enough about her workplace and her Customers to remain professional when on the job.

Customer service is, above all, an attitude. And a Customer-focused attitude is not something that can be turned on and off like a microphone switch. And speaking of switches . . . Heads up! Everyone has a recording device on their phones and tablets.

It's not switch happens but Shift Happens!® when companies do not consciously manage the Customer Experience.

DATING Your Customer®

Dazzle Customers with your Service. The key to good Customer Service is to treat all your Customers well, but not necessarily the same. Respond to each of your Customer's needs as an individual. While one Customer might need a ton of help and attention, another might prefer an opportunity to browse in privacy. Learn to understand body language and to read between the lines. It's up to you to perceive your Customers' Service preferences and to give each one of your Customers what they want.

Anticipate the needs of your Customers by emphasizing Service over sales. Good Service sells. But pushy Service people who are always trying to sell more can be a major turn-off to all your Customers. Whenever you are trying to sell something, only one question is on your Customer's mind: "Why are you trying to sell me something?"

Your Customers could come to two possible conclusions. First, they might believe you're trying to sell them something simply to get more revenue for yourself. Or, second, your Customers might believe you're trying to sell them something because you're interested in them, care about their needs, and are sincerely trying to help them. Anticipating the needs of your Customers can create long-term relationships that can help you sell them on ideas (rather than just products) by sharing your proven case histories with them. You can also help make your Customers' research for a resource an enjoyable experience.

Treat your Customers well by being a problem solver. If you can't help your Customers, help them find someone who can. Customers appreciate your help—especially when you aren't directly profiting from a sale. Consider this Service as an investment. Your Customers will appreciate the advice. They'll also remember you the next time they need your goods or your kind of Customer Service.

Innovate by understanding most rules should be flexible. Make sure you never say "No, that's against the rules" to a Customer who's making a reasonable request. Your main rule—one that should never be compromised—is to keep your Customers happy and satisfied.

Nurture your employees by giving them the care and respect you want them to give your Customers. If you treat your employees well, they will, in turn, be great ambassadors of care. If you treat them poorly, they'll treat your Customers the same way. A dissatisfied employee can't satisfy a Customer.

Remember, your employees are the center of gravity in your business because they are the ones who come in contact with your Customers, your products, and your Customer Service. If your employees are happy with your company, they can make others happy as well. Make your employees know they're important.

Guarantee both your employees and your Customers stay with you by making sure you have a great Customer Service Policy and that your employees understand and follow it. Try posting your Customer Service Policy in a central location for all to see. Once your employees understand the importance of great Customer Service, you'll have Customers returning over and over again.

According to Jim:
It's all about U. Is it UNIQUE, URGENT, USEFUL, ULTRASPECIFIC, and UNDERSTANDABLE from your Customers' perspective?

D Is for DAZZLE

Dazzle Your Customer with These 24 Principles That Accelerate the Achievement of Exceptional Customer Service

***Customer Service isn't a department.
Customer Service is an attitude.***

Great Customer Service helps you create an invisible advantage.

Learn what it takes to become the leader in your chosen field, to have satisfied Customers tell others why they should do business with you, and to be successful in everything you do.

Impress your Customers. What must you do this instant to begin developing Customer Retention? How can you take assertive command of your financial future? How can you help your Customers want to do business with you? Just like the first date, you aren't going to get a second chance to make a first impression.

If you demand the experience of living life to the fullest, delivering a quality product, and offering exceptional Customer Service, this begins with a commitment to *prevent* serious Customer Service issues before they develop.

If you Dazzle your Customer in the first place, then you'll never have to deal with Customer complaints you can't handle quickly. Believing you can prevent every complaint would be foolish, but you can certainly commit—with passion and focus on solutions that have one goal—to bring the Customer back.

"Our Customers are not there to field-test our products."
—Stanley C. Gault, chairman, Rubbermaid

If you establish Service systems that work in the first place, then you identify a Customer's specific complaint before it becomes a major issue. You deal with the complaint in time to prevent your Customer from becoming upset, hostile, or disruptive.

Remember your first date?

Remember how you thought about what to do, what to wear, how to act?

Remember getting enough courage to ask for the date?

Did you anticipate rejection?

If so, did you have a plan for your counter response?

Did you have a goal? Certainly. To get a date!

And what is the goal of great Customer Service?

To get and keep your Customer!

When you misinterpret your Customer's needs, this can sabotage your ability to give the best Service to your Customer. No matter how sincere you are, your attempts to create great Customer Service could be unsuccessful if you don't interpret your Customer's reaction correctly. You can never anticipate Customer reaction accurately. Simply being authentic isn't enough. To succeed, you must consider how you'll be interpreted.

Trying to understand the opposite sex enables us to make choices and decisions conducive to getting what we want, but also in a way that works.

In John Gray's book, *Mars and Venus on a Date: A Guide for Navigating the 5 Stages of Dating to Create a Loving and Lasting Relationship,* he says dating has five stages:

1. Attraction
2. Uncertainty
3. Exclusivity
4. Intimacy
5. Engagement

"Knowing what to expect in each of the five stages of dating makes it incredibly easier."

—John Gray, PhD

And so it begins. You see someone and you want to get to know that person better. No matter how experienced you are, the early stages of dating are uncomfortable and awkward for most of us. But, to find your soul mate, to find a significant other, this process is necessary.

> "When our relationships make sense to us, we don't make as many mistakes and are thus released from making the same mistakes again and again" (*Mars and Venus on a Date*, page 7).
>
> —John Gray, PhD

What is the ultimate objective of the first date?

To create a positive dating experience that leads to a second date.

And so on . . . until you've found out enough to make a decision that could impact the rest of your life. Customer Service is the same.

What prevents Customer complaints from escalating? Planning and communication. You can never prevent anyone from complaining, but you can prevent the escalation of complaints.

According to Jim:

Great Customer Service is like losing weight. Everyone is talking about it. Few are doing it. And those who actually give Customer Service aren't doing it well.

Businesses are losing Customers every day because they aren't talking the Customer Service talk . . . they aren't treating Customers the way they say they will. And their competitors love it.

When you were in high school, did you want to go out with the head cheerleader or the captain of the football team? Ever wonder how someone who wasn't as attractive, or well mannered, or even as good a dancer as you ended up going to the prom with your special someone?

Do you ever wonder how a company sells a similar product for more money than you do or has a product that isn't as innovative as yours gets more business? Did you suggest changes to your organization only to be informed that "not invented here" thinking creates roadblocks instead of bridges?

"Rid yourself of psychic vampires. Don't listen to those who say you can't, and find those who say you can."
—Tim Gard, CPAE, CSP Professional Speaker

Focus—Energy—Commitment

Great companies deliver on what they promise. They exceed Customer expectations. They have learned from their mistakes or from the mistakes of others. Look around you. Can you find many companies that offer great Service? Are they market leaders? Do others emulate them?

What can you learn from Nordstrom, Lexus, and Federal Express that you can apply to your own business? What can you learn from those companies that forgot the Customer is the reason they're in business? Look at the burial grounds filled with companies that had great products and lousy Service.

Target Your Customers.

Think of great Customer Satisfaction as hitting the bull's-eye of the target.

Each ring moving out from the bull's-eye means you're less and less targeted in your efforts. The further from the bull's-eye, the greater the likelihood your Customer will find some other resource to take care of their needs.

Remember how you missed the target the first time you shot at it?

- Did you learn how to correct your mistake? Did you benefit from the information and try again?
- Did you acknowledge you were aiming too far in one direction and, the next time, aim more in the other direction?
- Trial and error.

Eventually, you hit the target.

But, unless you're target shooting with bows and arrows or guns, here's how you can learn to hit the target: find companies with great Customer Service and copy them. Use their ideas. Replicate their success, and your company can avoid much wasted time and effort. Repeat what works!

You owe it to your Customer.

Great products with terrible Service won't keep you in business.

Great Service with mediocre products won't work either.

You need both to survive today.

You must know yourself and the abilities of those in your company to fulfill the needs of your Customers.

"Quality is the only patent protection we've got."
—James D. Robinson III, CEO,
American Express Corporation

Pilots file a flight plan. They plot each step along the route to get from point A to point B.

Pilots don't get into the plane without a flight plan, radio, fuel check, and so forth.

Build your plan the same way.

Your course is determined by the decisions you make and how you deal with problems.

You wouldn't fly a plane without a compass. And you shouldn't do business without having a plan to enable you to weather Customer Service issues that are simply part of doing business.

Two dozen ideas follow to help you dazzle your Customers before they express any concerns about your products or Service. Just like the first date, plan ahead. The results will be worth it.

"Really, we have hundreds of thousands of salespeople. They are our Customers. If you can't please your current Customers, you don't deserve the new ones."
—Scott D. Cook, founder of Intuit and creator of the successful personal finance-software program, Quicken

Diffuse

6) You have only one chance to make a first impression.

Dating requires punctuality, eye contact, conversation, and attention.

You open doors, pull out chairs, take charge, and make the best impression you can. Your grooming is perfect, your clothes are pressed, and your breath is fresh. Customers, like dates, go where they feel welcome and appreciated.

When you're on a first date, you have great eye contact. You don't let your date feel invisible. You don't spend time looking at other people or answering your cell phone. All your attention is focused on the delivery of a message: "I am the best choice you could make. I am the one you want to be with." People always put up with little disappointments if you act like you know they're there.

A Customer might be disappointed with a delay and the lack of delivery.

A Customer can get angry at the bad treatment they continue to receive.

The goal of great Customer Service should be to intervene at the earliest possible stage.

Dough

7) You owe it to your Customer—the one who has chosen to give their hard-earned money to your business.

Customers demand, and Customers deserve, the best you have to offer. You'll never get the second date if the first one isn't thought out well. Dazzle your date. Dazzle your Customer. Average simply doesn't make the cut.

Know your outcome.

> **A REMINDER:**
>
> No matter what your business, your Customers come first.
>
> Here's a real-world example:
>
> From Karl's Party Rental's newsletter . . .
>
> Spring is upon us and you know what that means. It's event-planning time! Whether you are planning a graduation, wedding, festival, or any type of event, Karl's Party Rental is THE place to call for all your party rental needs. We are always adding new items to our inventory, and this spring we have been busy recruiting, hiring, and training many new employees to be able to meet all our Customer's delivery and set-up needs.
>
> Each new employee attends an orientation session to become acclimated to all of Karl's policies and regulations. Then, practical training sessions are conducted at the warehouse before the employee is out on the job site. Our philosophy is that training is an ongoing process and much is also learned while on the job. Our crew leaders are always willing to share their knowledge with the new person. So, while you may see many new faces this summer, you will receive the same excellent care you have come to expect from Karl's.

Dollars

8) You owe it to your company—the one that not only pays you money, but also entrusts you with its livelihood and future.

Your company deserves the best you have to offer. A date is a relationship. Both of you have certain expectations. Exceeding those expectations gets you another date. **Know your purpose.** To understand the actual "dollar economics" of your Customer, you must know two values. You must know each of these values and understand their relationship to each other. First, your organization must know the cost to obtain and retain a new Customer. And, second, you must know their lifetime value. What will your Customer spend during the lifetime of their involvement with your company? If you learn nothing else from this manual, learn this:

> **You must know the exact cost to obtain and retain a new Customer, as well as the exact lifetime value of that Customer.**

According to Jim:

Let me repeat that. The cost to obtain and acquire a new Customer and their lifetime value are the two most important quantities of economic awareness necessary to the success of your organization.

Dinero

9) **You owe it to yourself—the one who enjoys the pride, satisfaction, and reputation that comes from giving your all.**

Your date deserves the best you have to offer. What's the worst that can happen on the first date? You find out you have nothing in common. You learn the other person is simply not who you're looking for. So what? You've learned valuable information and benefited from the experience. And, if it was a good experience, you'll share it with others.

According to Jim:

Are you proud enough to buy what you build?

"I just found a wonderful website. It offers products at fair prices and great Service. Check it out."

People love to mentor others. How often have you told someone about a movie you thought they'd like, even though you didn't care for it? How often have you found a good restaurant and told others? Before you recycle the next junk mail brochure, ask yourself if you know someone who might find it useful.

**"Never forget—
the Customer owns the store."**

—Sam Walton, Wal-Mart

Remember, people trust their friends. Friends always try to become a resource of timely, valuable information. The mentoring process is omnipotent. Other people's experience is fundamental in any business or social environment. We all try to learn from others' successes and mistakes.

Differ

10) Understand your Customer's needs and expectations . . . instead of trying to talk your way through the sale or excuse.

What you really want is consistent results. If you dazzle your Customer in the first place, your chance of having a bad Customer Service experience is reduced.

People like to forgive. Admit the mistake and offer a solution. In providing the solution, you create rapport that can dazzle your Customer.

> "I went into a restaurant during the day, a restaurant I had good experiences in on several occasions in the evening. What a difference with a different crew during the day. I discovered no soap in the men's room, asked the waitress for soap, she checked with another waitress who in irritation said that it was not the day in which the soap was replaced by some outside vendor. The waitress relayed the message

to me. I then asked for soap from the kitchen and was told that was not possible. I asked if I could have a bit of the dishwashing soap and I was told no. I asked at that point in a calm voice if they washed dishes? At that point, the senior waitress became involved and told me to use the women's room, that there may be soap there. There was, but I have not returned to that restaurant since."

—Tom Burns

Dream

11) Treat your Customers the way you want to be treated.

Dreams are developed because we all want to be treated well. It's the better Service, not the better product, that makes the difference. It's the best relationship, not the lowest price. The good-looking guy may turn many heads, but more women marry for sensitivity, caring, and warmth rather than for great pecs or abs, or a handsome face. Sure, we all look at great bodies and, as Customers, at fancy products, that offer flash, packaging, and advertising. Once you've been sold on their visual appeal, however, is their delivery what was promised?

Customers like to be told they have good taste. Customers like attention.

Dazzle them!

According to Jim:
What should follow is you would never let a Customer's problem escalate beyond disappointment.

Differentiate

12) Look directly in the eyes of your Customer or your date.

Thinking about someone or something else is difficult if you're looking and listening face-to-face.

Doing this shows you're interested. It shows you care. Customers are "Ma'am" or "Sir" if you feel using their first name is inappropriate. The sooner you gain permission to call a Customer by their first name, though, the sooner you make the interaction more friendly and personal. You have now connected person-to-person instead of station-to-station.

Depose

13) Honor the uniqueness of each Customer.

Take the time to understand your Customer's needs, issues, and concerns.

After your first date, did you kiss good night? Was there anticipation? Was there fear? What happened if you didn't kiss on the first date? As a man, you were thought a gentleman. As a woman, you might have felt relief. In both cases, anticipation for the first kiss still exists . . . **and that alone could get you a second date.**

Heather, a friend of mine, ordered a watch online. This was her first e-commerce experience. Heather was unsure about the process of using an online shopping cart and she wasn't comfortable about giving her credit card information on the Internet. But the site provided a price list, nice photos, and a description of the exact replica watch she wanted to give as a graduation present.

Heather ordered the watch using her credit card and the invoice came up with a $10 charge for 2nd day UPS Service. There was no way to delete it.

So, Heather let the unwanted charge go. The order was placed on May 11, for a gift she needed on May 27. Because the watch was supposed to arrive in two days, she wasn't concerned.

Heather left town on a business trip, fully confident that the watch would arrive in enough time for the graduation. When she returned on May 18 (seven days after the order), the watch hadn't arrived. Heather tried to call the company, but she couldn't reach anyone. She left a message on the company's voice mail. When Heather hadn't received a response on the following day, she called again. Again, no real person was available, so she left another voice mail. Heather sent her first email at 11 A.M., a second email at 3 P.M., and then she left another voice-mail message.

According to Jim:
What doesn't make sense is investing to attract new Customers, and then failing to match that effort with follow-through.

Following are email communications between Heather and the company:

On May 19, Heather wrote:

On the 11th of May I placed an order.
Your invoice 41706.
Panthère de Cartier watch Stainless steel white face.
The system required me to pay $10 extra for UPS 2nd day.
As of today, the order has not arrived.
Please advise by calling me at 312-527-xxxx or email at xxxxx@aol.com.
This was to be a gift at the end of this week.
Please make sure that I have the watch prior to close of business on Thursday. Thank you.

The company responded on May 22:

The day you ordered, someone sent me the love virus and it took almost three days to get my system back up and running. So we never even got your order. I will do my very best to get this to you ASAP. Thanks, ???????

The company wrote again on May 23:

If you have a copy of the order, I can ship it ASAP.
Thanks, ?????

Heather responded the same day:

Do you need another order?
If you lost the order, how do you know what to ship?
I ordered this in plenty of time to get here.
I am sorry you had a problem but, as you can understand, this is a gift and I need to be reassured it will arrive in time.
If you need more information, call me. Please confirm the watch will be here.

Later that afternoon, Heather wrote:

Today we received a charge for the watch. The order was processed on May 12. This is contrary to your statement that you lost the order due to a virus. How could you lose my order and still charge my credit card? In addition, you charged $139 and did not send the order.
This is a serious problem, which I expect to be resolved in my favor right away.
I suggest you call me and let me know what you have done to get me the order, and what you will do to remove the overcharge.

- The company promised to find the watch and ship it in time.
- The company never called.
- The company never shipped the watch.
- The company then sent emails that detailed how others were happy with their Service.
- The director of marketing got involved and promised to resolve the order within 24 hours.
- Five days later, still no watch or tracking number to show the watch had shipped.
- More emails, more promises. After an elapsed time of over 25 days from the original order date, still no watch. More emails and more promises. No results.
- Finally, a watch was received, a poorly packaged watch. No further follow up or letter was ever received from the company.

Ask yourself, am I going to continue to do business with a company that can't keep the promises they make? Don't I have other choices for companies that will make an effort to keep me as a Customer? Do I really want to D-A-T-E this company? More importantly, do such companies understand D-A-T-I-N-G?

As you look at the previous event, as well as the world events since the millennium, it's clear that change is the dominant factor. Our "for sures" are now being replaced with n speed and unfamiliar consequences. And, yet with the speed of opportunity; the mastery of new technology; social media growth; world-wide political unrest; and the mergers and acquisitions of brands, companies, and organizations, one constant exists: the need for Customers.

Dilate

14) Develop a relationship with each Customer before you address the Customer's request or attempt to make the sale or offer a resolution.

On the first date, you talk about general things. You discuss where you've lived and traveled, movies, music, television shows, homework, or traffic. You don't discuss politics, sex, or religion. This simply is inappropriate. The same with your initial contact with a Customer. Look and listen for, and then comment on things you have in common. Make the conversation as personable as possible. Pamper . . . go the extra mile to make it right.

Over decades of personal and official travel, Ed Slusarczyk has found that 99 percent of the time, the first and most important factor in establishing relationships anywhere in the world with a person from any background is establishing common ground.

> "This means engaging people in conversation about their families, especially their children, if they have any."
>
> —Ed Slusarczyk, owner of Ag Radio Network, which broadcasts on about 150 stations internationally

Direct

15) Give your Customer 100 percent of your attention.

Do the paperwork, cell phone calls, computer input, e-mails, or other issues on your own time, not on your Customer's time. What message are you sending when you accept that cell phone call instead of focusing on your Customer's needs?

Empathize . . . imagine yourself in your Customer's shoes. What can you do to meet their needs? What can you offer to help solve the problem?

How can you be the solution to, rather than the cause of, your Customer's problem?

> Southwest Airlines always capitalizes the word "Customer" whenever it's used in ads, brochures, annual reports, or other materials. (You've probably noticed I do the same. I started before Southwest was created because I believe in the importance of recognition of all Customers.) While this practice may seem picayune, what better way exists to flag employees and the public that the Customer really matters?

Discover

16) Listen more and talk less.

Listening is a lost art. Listen with your entire body. Listen so your Customer feels anything you say will have a serious impact on them. Listen with your eyes. Show your Customer you care.

Listening means you're focused on understanding your Customer's concern. Your Customer only needs to know what you're going to do to ease their problem.

According to Jim:
Customer complaints are the school books from which we learn some valuable lessons.

Deliver

17) Under-promise and over-deliver.

Make what you provide extraordinary.

This is a simple premise. If your Customer expectations are exceeded, then Customers will only complain if a real problem occurs. If your first date was well thought out and planned, a second date will most likely happen. Customer Service is about doing, not about explaining or rationalizing what you aren't doing.

**"We do not measure quality.
Quality is in the eyes of the Customer."**
—Steve Jobs, Apple Computer

Determination

18) Determination is what Customer Service is all about. Commit!

What business are you really in? Ask, and you will hear people say e-commerce, banking, insurance, automobile sales, healthcare, real estate, restaurant, entertainment, and so forth. It's the same when you ask someone out for a date. You say, "Would you like to go to a movie?" or, "Do you want to have a drink?" What you really mean is something different. What you really mean is, "I think getting to know you could lead to something special for both of us."

If all your Customers went to the competition, what business would you be in? If no one will date you, how can you find a significant other? In both cases, you want to dazzle. You want to impress. You want to meet any demands before the demands are made.

Digress

19) Recap the discussion.

Discuss what you've learned from that special person, not what you told them. Your goal is for the person to feel better about their decision to go out with you in the first place . . . or to do business with you.

Always thank your Customers. Tell your Customers how much you appreciate their choosing your business. Let them know you're committed to making their time with you well spent. Reaffirm your Customer's and your date's beliefs that you were a good choice in the first place.

Do!

20) Always invite your Customer to return.

Always set the tone for the next meeting.

Always close your interactions during the conversation with how much you appreciate your Customer. Give your Customer genuine appreciation.

A date is a test. You wanted to go out because you were interested in the other person. This interest may have been social, physical, intellectual, spiritual, or any combination thereof. This person might have been introduced to you by a friend, or you may have gone out for any number of reasons only you know. In any case, failure wasn't part of your plan.

Customers do business with a company because they think that firm is the best solution to their needs. Customers vote with their dollars. At no time do Customers think you'll fail or not deliver on what you promise. By the time Customers give you an order, they've gone through considerable evaluation and decided you are the best choice.

Any date starts with a raised level of expectations. No one goes out just to "kill time." A reason always exists. Most of us go out with someone because they have some quality we like. Perhaps the person has a delightful sense of humor. Maybe they're especially smart. It could be a physical attraction. Or, the person could have a magnetic personality. Something attracted you to accept the date. Discovering the compelling reason for the acceptance can make the entire experience more productive.

Detail

21) Look sharp. Listen sharp. Be sharp.

Nothing adds more power to your life than concentrating all your energies. "Look sharp" doesn't refer to how you dress. Dressing well is something anyone can do and it's expected. Look sharp means focusing all your energy on a goal: a repeat performance, a second date, more business.

"Listen sharp" is something we still don't do. We talk. Listening tells you how to act and how to react to anything. Listen sharp in everything you say and do, and respond in a concise, precise manner.

Listening sharp is an ever-present state of mind. Sharp means attentive. "Being sharp" is what Anthony ("Tony") Robbins calls the "peak state." "Being at your peak state" means being at the top of your game, ready for anything life throws at you. Words represent 7 percent of what actually influences human behavior. Voice qualities offer another 33 percent. How you use your voice can affect someone more than what you say.

Using your body language represents a majority of what influences someone when you communicate. All emotions are concentrated on being sharp.

Now think about when you were dating.

Did you listen?
Did you observe?
Were you "sharp" on the first date?
The second?
The third?
Did anything change?
During the first few dates, did you ask a lot of questions?
Did you mentally records your observations? Sure you did!

You learned of your date's dreams, wants, desires, expectations, and values.

If you had many first, second, and third dates during your lifetime, you found none of them were the same. You became an expert at isolating their true motivations and expectations.

That same process applies to D-A-T-I-N-G Your Customer®.

Dredge

22) Have energy. Show energy. Deliver energy.

Knowing how to concentrate and focus energy on important things is important, instead of frittering your energy away on trivia. Formulate a strategy. Check your strategy. Change it. Constantly measure the results. Learn from your mistakes. Assess what the plan is doing for you. Continue to deliver your message by learning what works and what doesn't.

Domesticate

23) Focus your full attention on what you have a burning desire to achieve.

See the end results. What do you love to do? What are you best at doing?

What really drives you in life? In business? For your next date? People always do the best they can with the resources they have in their toolbox.

Learn how to do what drives you better. Focus all your energy on achieving the goals you set for yourself and your company. Frail Japanese karate experts put their hands through bricks. Amazing feats are recorded daily from those who do extraordinary things because they focused on the goal. You're only trying to dazzle someone. How difficult can that be?

Demand

24) Drive to make your achievement possible.

Be single-minded. Customers are like dates. They want to be reassured that their decision is correct. They want to know you care. They want you to be honest, caring, and committed to making each contact better than the last one. Ask how your Customers were motivated. Ask for feedback. You might be surprised, but you should be prepared for new information. Don't overreact. Take the information and evaluate what you've learned. Listen for specific triggers that your Customers feel positively motivated them. Also ask for any negative feelings, so you can avoid them in the future. Become the best in the world at what you do. Commit to making a quantum leap in your willingness to dazzle your Customers.

According to Jim:
Customer Service is just like D ◊ A ◊ T ◊ I ◊ N ◊ G. The objective of both is to get a second date.

- Deliver WOW through Service.
- Embrace and Drive Change.
- Create Fun and A Little Weirdness.
- Be Adventurous, Creative, and Open-Minded.
- Pursue Growth and Learning.
- Build Open and Honest Relationships With Communication.
- Build a Positive Team and Family Spirit.
- Do More With Less.
- Be Passionate and Determined.
- Be humble.
- Be willing to fail but learn from it.
- Make Shift Happen.

Digest

25) Gather in your resources, rally all your faculties, marshal all your energies, and focus all your abilities on mastering your field of endeavor, exceeding your Customer's expectations.

Learning is a relationship between the unknown and the known. Fortunately, your Customers and your dates offer you guidance whether or not you want it! Most of the time, your Customers tell or show you what's wrong. If you're attentive, you also learn what's right. In either case, you can formulate a strategy that helps you organize your information and resources. This enables you to produce a specific result consistently . . . dazzling them.

A simple philosophy turned this family's seed business into a household name. "I always try to remember," Burpee said, "that people really aren't interested in my seeds. They're interested in their gardens, their tomatoes, and their lawns."
—David Burpee, known by gardeners throughout the world

According to Jim:
It's the product of the product that people purchase, not the product itself.

Duplicate

26) Repeat what works for you.

By listening and watching, you can tell what gets a positive response. Find a common ground. Make that common ground your goal and replicate those areas that get the most positive response. You want to be able to duplicate anything you've done that accomplished the goal you set for yourself. Remember the first time you got that special date? Remember your first really big order? What did you do to get it? How did you act? What did you say? Look around you. Do you know someone who gets the kind of results you want? Do you see someone who has developed a skill you admire? Do you see great Customer Service around you? When you do, create an environment of uninterrupted focus. Develop habits to attain and maintain your peak state, so you continue to dazzle your Customers.

Drill

27) Create a toolbox.

You'll soon learn what works and what doesn't.

Just as traditional flowers and candy seem to work well for any date, you can reinforce your relationship with a Customer prior to starting business with them. Identify what your Customer wants and deliver it.

Keep accurate records of what worked. Get names and dates that can have a meaningful impact in the future. Take notes. All of this shows you care. Write down the information and read it back to your Customer. Confirm. Reconfirm. Make sure you set up a calming atmosphere that can be replicated. Experiment, but don't take unnecessary risks.

Delight

28) Reinforce your Customer's decision to be with you.

Make your Customer feel their time was well spent and the decision to be with you was a wise one. Never let a Customer regret a decision. Thank your Customer. If your Customer isn't satisfied, they will find someone else. Ask your Customer directly, "How was our Customer Service?" Set the groundwork for the next experience. Don't let any Customers leave without making sure they know you want to continue working with them. The goal is always to have your Customers return.

> Consider Japan's 100-year-old Shiseido, now the world's fourth largest cosmetic company. Japanese consumers are particularly demanding when it comes to refreshed products, sometimes expecting updated offerings as frequently as every month. As Akira Gemma, the President of Shiseido, says, "We see our Customers as our own competitors. We need to move ahead not because other brands are doing so, but because our Customer's needs are changing."
>
> —Harvard Business Review

Draft

29) Think "relationship."

A date or a business relationship is the same.

Each expects something in return. A date expects a pleasant experience.

Good company. A reasonable attempt to make the date pleasant.

If the expectations are exceeded, another date might occur. The same with your Customer. If your business relationship is satisfying, Customers reward you with more business and more referrals.

At the beginning, your goal is short-term. The rapport you establish should lead to a long-term relationship. Every transaction or date is a comparison of another. There's a ranking . . . for better or worse. If it's better, the relationship might continue. If not, little incentive exists to continue. Surprises are welcome. Flattery is expected. Nothing in life has any meaning except the meaning a person gives to it. Business and social relationships are similar. The quality of both is influenced by the communication skills and reception of the other person. Your ultimate goal is to create relationship-building.

When your Customers find you invaluable and indispensable, they'll overlook occasional errors, much the same as a date who ignores your occasional blunder. Customers are all you have. Every decision, every action, every thought you make must be based on this awareness.

> "The challenge is to get people to willingly do more than they would, to rise above the norm, to perform at their highest levels of potential."
>
> —General H. Norman Schwarzkopf, Jr., Commander of Allied Forces, Gulf War

The sun's rays don't burn until they're brought to a focus.

The same is true with great Customer Service. Don't talk about it . . . Do it! Don't think about it . . . Do it! Don't read about it . . . Do it! Like the ad says, "Just do it!"

D-A-T-I-N-G requires a process of learning what works and what doesn't. I learned early that even if I didn't want the dating relationship to continue, I needed to make my way through the tough process of acknowledging my wishes and be respectful of how that might impact others. Customers, like dates, talk to their friends. If the experience was good, they share it. If the experience was bad, they tweet it, email it, Instagram it, Facebook it, and maybe even blog about it. Rudeness is a certain path to destruction.

Comcast makes it to the top of my worst Customer Service experiences. As Comcast has grown larger, the company has distanced itself from its Customers. Almost every day, I get a letter from Comcast asking me to use their business Services. What Comcast apparently didn't realize is I was already their business Customer. But I found Comcast had a total disregard for my business needs, so I dropped them. It took several billing periods, dozens of written and voice complaints, and constant frustration at their inability to respond in a timely manner. I understand Comcast now has 130,000 employees, but that isn't an excuse.

Comcast changed a Customer's name to "Asshole" Brown after he tried to cancel his cable package and another Chicago-area Customer found she had been renamed "Bitch Dog" by the cable company. Need more proof? Read this report:

"Comcast Does It Again and Renames a Customer 'SuperBitch' Bauer"[1]

"Yesterday Mary Bauer received her Comcast bill in the mail. But the 63-year-old Chicago area resident says she's not going to open it. That's because someone at Comcast switched her name on the bill, addressing it instead to 'SuperBitch Bauer.'"

Bauer has been having problems with Comcast for months. As she related her story to Chicago's WGN television station, she's had a lot of Service and billing issues. Technicians have been dispatched to her place a whopping 39 times, and she recently got into it with telephone support after her bills stopped arriving. Comcast uses "retention specialists," but the company continues to fail at the basics of any dating relationship . . . keeping the focus on Service.

If your employees aren't happy, they can't make your Customer happy. How can any organization allow this kind of behavior? Simple! It starts from the top down. As Comcast (and the cable television business) has consolidated, cable television providers are most often on the Top 10 List of Worst Customer Service Companies. With the reduced competition in the marketplace, many Customers complain about the reduced Service level from cable and satellite providers. In a world defined by electronic interfaces, honest face-to-face Customer Service is even more crucial. If no competition exists and if there are no choices, Customers must accept mediocrity. This is what's becoming more typical as consolidations, mergers, and the cost of entry for new competitors navigate the seas of change. After all, Shift Happens!®

Once Customers have been blinded by your presence, they'll want to face the light and enjoy your radiance. Dazzle them . . . and they'll return.

It's just like DATING. No one else can be you or do what you do.

DATING proves that it's not always the more handsome or beautiful who are the best dates. Often, it's someone who makes laugher part of the "package." High school crushes are often about image, or popularity, or athletic status, but long-term dating is seldom based on those superficial traits alone.

At this writing Tom Karinshak is the Senior Vice President of Customer Experience. I have personally written and called his office only to receive dozens of replies from "his office" and a different person

---

1 By Robert McMillan 02.05.15 http://www.wired.com/2015/02/comcast-renames-customer-superbitch-bauer/

on almost each response. Using "cut and paste," Tom is apparently too busy to talk to the Customers he promised to serve.[2]

Three Levels of Anger

While Customers might sometimes be disappointed in the quality of a product they purchase, they get angry when they're treated badly or unfairly. The level of anger escalates as follows:

Level One is disappointment.

It didn't arrive. It doesn't work.
I call the company or write to them. Nothing happens.

Level Two is frustration.

The company doesn't respond.
It makes promises it doesn't keep.

Level Three is anger.

Thinking: I'm so angry at how that company is treating me, I'm going to take my business elsewhere.
Feeling: This is ridiculous. I'm getting even angrier. I feel like making them as miserable as I am.
Doing: They can't treat me this way. I'm going to write a letter. I'm going to tell everyone I can.

Never let a problem escalate beyond disappointment.

You can't run a business from the backroom. You must get into the market and meet your Customer. The *center of gravity* for your business is where your Customer is located.

The perspective from the Customers' point-of-view is different than yours.

Do whatever it takes to keep a Customer.

Sometimes it costs money.
Sometimes it isn't worth it.
What can you do to keep your Customer happy?

---

[2] https://www.facebook.com/xfinity/posts/10151945823904056

Commit to becoming a front-line manager.

Try being your own Customer.
Talk to your Customers.
E-mail your Customers.
Take a personal interest in every one of your Customers.

Treat Customers as if you were the Customer!

Work at developing a relationship before you address the Customer's request, attempt to make the sale, or offer a resolution.

Honor the uniqueness of each of your Customers.

Take the time to understand your Customer's needs, issues, and concerns.

Ask satisfied Customers, "How did we do?"

Ask dissatisfied Customers, "How can I resolve this to your satisfaction?"

The single most important word: Yes!

The two most important words to a Customer: Thank You!

Make Customer Service a part of all written or verbal job descriptions, no matter what the function or level.

Everyone in the company is in the Customer Service business.

> "Motivate them, train them, care about them, and make winners out of them . . . we know that if we treat our employees correctly, they'll treat the Customers right. And if Customers are treated right, they'll come back."
>
> —J. W. Marriott, Jr., Chairman, Marriott Hotels and Resorts

Focus on the people who focus on the Customers.
This means everyone in your organization.
And, if you are the manager . . .

1. Commit to at least two hours each month working alongside everyone who comes in contact with your Customers. You'll be amazed at what you can learn. Adopt a policy of returning calls and email within the same business day. Respond to all email with, at least, a timetable of a response. (Thank you for your email. It will take me until xx p.m. to research your request and offer you a resolution. If you have

time, though, perhaps you can assist me in providing a suggestion. From your standpoint, how can I resolve this matter to your satisfaction and keep you as a Customer?)
2. Go on a Debilitating Policy Hunt. Ask everyone to identify policies and procedures that get in the way of providing good Service. Then, do your best to update, modify, or eliminate as many as you can (for example, reread Heather's memo regarding freight charges).
3. Recognize and reward employees who provide exceptional Customer Service. Share their stories with others. This can motivate your entire team. A dissatisfied employee can't satisfy a Customer. Motivated employees go above and beyond for your Customers . . . and for your organization.

According to Jim:
Being your own Customer on a regular basis is something you must do to become Customer-driven.

A Crash Course On Customer Service: The MOST important word:

Action Summary

Customers can be a mystery .... UNFOLD IT!

Customers are sometimes a struggle .... FACE IT!

Customer relationships can be beautiful............ PRAISE IT!

Customer Service is sometimes a puzzle............. SOLVE IT!

Customers always present an opportunity......... TAKE IT!

Customers are like a song .... SING IT!

Customers demand great Service .... ACHIEVE IT!

Customers reward you with repeat business...... FULFILL IT!

Remember, D ❧ A ❧ T ❧ I ❧ N ❧ G Is Fun!

According to Jim:

The marketplace looks totally different from where your Customer is standing. Make all decisions from your Customer's perspective.

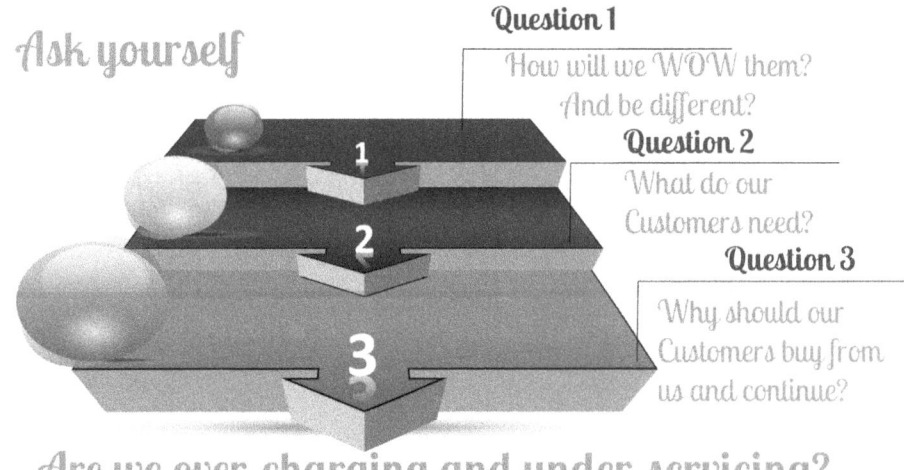

Ask yourself

Question 1
How will we WOW them? And be different?

Question 2
What do our Customers need?

Question 3
Why should our Customers buy from us and continue?

Are we over-charging and under-servicing?

24 Dazzling Ideas

1. You only have one chance to make a first impression.
2. You owe it to your Customer.
3. You owe it to your company.
4. You owe it to yourself.
5. Understand your Customer's needs and expectations.
6. Treat your Customers the way you want to be treated.
7. Look directly in the eyes of your Customer.
8. Honor the uniqueness of each Customer.
9. Develop a relationship with each Customer.
10. Give your Customer 100 percent of your attention.
11. Listen more and talk less to your Customer.
12. Under-promise and over-deliver to your Customer.
13. Determination is what Customer Service is all about.
14. Recap the discussion.
15. Always invite your Customer to return.
16. Look sharp. Listen sharp. Be sharp.
17. Have energy. Show energy. Deliver energy.
18. Focus your full attention on what you have a burning desire to achieve.
19. Drive to make your achievement possible.
20. Gather in your resources.
21. Repeat what is working for you.
22. Create a toolbox.
23. Reinforce your Customer's decision to be with you.
24. Think "relationship."

Dating Your Customer®

A Is for ANTICIPATE

25 Ways to Anticipate the Needs of Your Customers by Emphasizing Service over Sales Anticipate

"We must obey the great law of change. It is the most powerful law of nature."

—Edmund Burke

In today's world, the only constant is change. With rare exception, participating in life is difficult without being touched by change. Change permeates our personal lives, our business world, our government, and beyond. Every time you have a date or attend a social event with your significant other, emotions and expectations come into play. While you can't be a mind reader, if you initially dazzle your partner, minor differences should be forgotten quickly. Remember, dating is just like keeping a Customer happy. You need to dazzle your partner or your Customer in the first place, and then anticipate their needs and wants.

Think for a moment of products and Services that weren't in common use a decade ago. Think about how they've affected our lives. Cellular phones, personal pagers, modems, fax machines, CD-ROMs, personal computers, the Internet, email, voice mail, and satellite dishes all have revolutionized the way we transmit and receive information. Microwave ovens have altered the speed with which we can prepare food, and the Food Service industry has responded with new packaging and portions.

No sector of our lives has gone unchanged—there's no escaping change!

Accept

1) Don't resist the idea of change—or the implementation of change.

We all desperately hold on to the way we've always done things . . . even if we don't know why we're doing it.

We do things "the same old way" because this gives us a feeling of control over our lives and some measure of comfort or security. But, just like the proverbial ostrich burying its head in the sand, ignoring or resisting change won't stop it. Change starts when someone sees the next step.

> **"Things ain't what they ought to be. Things ain't what they gonna be. But thank God things ain't like they was."**
>
> —Adage

Acknowledge

2) Embrace change and manage it the best way you can.

This means having an open mind, learning new skills and behaviors, and having the willingness to change.

As a microcosm of the world, corporate America is as vulnerable to change as any individual. We witness this in the form of restructuring, reengineering, total quality management initiatives, downsizing, resizing, acquisitions, and mergers. And many of these efforts fail to change. So, too, do many attempts to make personal changes. How many of us exercise regularly, follow healthier diets, lower our blood pressure, spend more quality time with our families, end a bad marriage or job, or fail to quit smoking or drinking?

Change Requires:
- ♥ Courage
- ♥ Heart
- ♥ Adaptability
- ♥ Nurturing
- ♥ Grace
- ♥ Energy

Agree

3) View change as a process.

In part, failures to change stem from viewing change as an end result. Change can be seen as all or nothing, now or never. By approaching change in this way, we invariably fail. Instead, we need to view change as a process. Customers change their minds. Products don't always meet expectations.

Many years ago, when my mother gave me two ties as a gift, I immediately knew I couldn't please her. I went into my room and put on one of the ties. When I came out to show her how great the tie looked, she said, "What's the matter? You don't like the other one?"

In the broad scope of change, mothers are really no different than dates or Customers. We spend our lives trying to please them. Sometimes it works and, other times, it doesn't. Mothers, like a great date, though, are forgiving. And, like the weather, they often change without notice. We need to understand that change is a process and we are all part of that process. To try to understand change fully, you must accept the fact that change itself alters its course. Our job is to accept change and try to move with it, instead of against it.

So, I told my mother the tie I had chosen to wear went better with the shirt and slacks I was wearing because they were her favorites. And I suggested she view the tie in combination with my outfit, instead of only as which tie I had chosen to wear.

> **"It's not a failure. What we're doing is just delaying another success."**
>
> —Commander Frank L. Culbertson, Jr., of Space Shuttle Discovery, after the fourth launch delay came seconds before liftoff

Consider an example provided by a well-known celebrity. Oprah Winfrey has waged a battle with her weight for many years. At her highest weight, Oprah weighed 237 pounds; at her lowest weight, she weighed 142 pounds. But even though Oprah reached her goal, she couldn't sustain the change and, ultimately, she regained the weight. She failed.

Then Oprah met a man whose approach to changing her problem was totally different. Bob Greene helped Oprah to understand and focus on the reasons why she ate the way she did, not just how and what she ate. Once Oprah truly understood the role of food in her life—a comfort, a way to avoid feelings, a reaction to stress, something she could control, and so forth—she began to change her behavior. In addition to eating more carefully, Oprah incorporated regular exercise, and other means of rebalancing and renewal.

Oprah didn't do everything all at once. The change was a process, one step at a time. As Oprah gained awareness and confidence, she attempted the next step. Oprah finally succeeded in making the change she'd wanted for so many years, but now she realizes this reasoning sounds warped. Oprah says that's what the ego does. "[Ego] is sick. It's wily, it's cunning, it's deceptive. It's an impostor imposing on the real you," Oprah said. "You're not the shape of your body. You're not your status. You're not your position in life. You're not the car you drive, no matter how fancy it is. You're not your house or your square footage."

And now Oprah owns Weight Watchers.

Acclimate

4) View the process of change as a moving target.

While you'll never get control of the process, you can understand how to cope with the results.

When a tidal wave hits land, three basic responses occur:

The first group of people say, "I've seen it all before." They do nothing and they are drowned.

The second group of people say, "I'm getting out of here!" They hide and their businesses are destroyed.

And the third group of people say, "This is a tidal wave. I'd better learn to surf."

This manual teaches you to surf in the face of the challenges ahead.

After all, if you're not riding the wave of change, you could find yourself beneath it. Shift Happens!® to all of us. Either you're creating shift or shift is managing you.

> **"It was not long ago that people thought semiconductors were part-time orchestra leaders and microchips were very, very small snack foods."**
>
> —Geraldine A. Ferraro

Act Out

Line up ten people in a straight line and ask them to pretend they're a production line or a sports team. Give them twelve balls of different colors. Explain that everyone must touch each ball before it's tossed in a bin. The object is to do this exercise in the least amount of time possible.

The game proceeds as follows: the first person to touch the ball hands it to the next person, who hands it to the next person, and so on. The last person to touch the ball hands it back to the first person, who then places it in a container in the middle of the line. When all twelve balls are in the bin, the clock stops and the time is recorded.

Next, ask the team to come up with its own method of moving the balls, with the goal to cut its time by 50 percent. Then, give the team two tries. Typically, the team will repeat exactly the same process and shave a bit off its time in the second and third attempts.

After the third attempt, change the order in which the team members are standing and, without any discussion, ask the team to try again. It's quite likely this fourth attempt will be chaos and the team won't be able to match its best times.

The only thing changed is the order in which the people are standing. But the perception is one of total disruption, which markedly affects the performance outcome. The exercise reflects what happens in the real world. Just when you think things are going well, management, the government, or your family changes the rules, and you don't know how to cope. Shift Happens!®

This same phenomenon occurs in the marketplace. A change in one department might have absolutely no real impact on the rest of the organization, but it could be perceived as affecting operations. This is a key distinction. Often, nothing has changed significantly—only your perception of reality has changed. And the most important perception is that of your Customer. If your Customer believes something changed, for better or worse, this is all that matters. Arguing or trying to change the perception is pointless. Your role is to make the best of the perception. After all, perception is reality.

In the exercise, one brave soul might suggest the group change the physical structure from a line to a circle, tight enough so everyone can touch the ball simultaneously, instead of one at a time. This individual may explain that because the ball never leaves the hands of the first person, that person is automatically the last to touch it and can immediately drop it in the container. This improves the performance time dramatically, which is the stated goal, while still adhering to the original rules.

> **"In the future, the only sustainable competitive advantage will become the ability to learn faster than one's competition."**
>
> —Arie de Geus, formerly of Royal Dutch Shell, now a visiting fellow at the London Business School

Accommodate

5) Your Customers *always* think they're right.

Don't try to change the mind of your Customers. While it might seem obvious that every group would immediately see the wisdom in the suggestion and adopt the change, this isn't the case. Members of the team will come up with all sorts of reasons why it won't work, why they can't do it, and so forth. Don't let yourself find the reasons you can't accommodate your Customer's request.

This happens all the time in the market place. The long-range performance goal or the short-term strategy hasn't changed; the only thing that's changed is the means of reaching it. Rather than panicking or resisting change, you need to assess what is perception and what is reality, and then adapt accordingly.

Ever had an argument with your significant other? Ever been really upset? Have you come into the room ready for battle, stated your case, and heard, "You're right, honey. I'm so sorry. Please forgive me."

Now what? Because you thought you were right and the other person agreed, the argument is over. You might think differently, but there's no point in doing anything but trying to accommodate that person's need to be right.

Sometimes, as demonstrated in the game, this means mastering new skills, behaviors, and working relationships. It isn't easy. Nobody said it was easy . . . but it can be fun! The rewards are fantastic.

"It's all right to be Goliath, but always act like David."
—Phil Knight, Founder, President, and CEO of Nike

Adjust

6) Managing during periods of change often requires changing yourself.

Your old managerial skills and behaviors might no longer prove effective in a changed work environment—the "cut off part of the ham before you put it in the oven" syndrome.

If you want to be successful in getting others to take risks and to learn new skills and behaviors, you must be willing to change the way you work and deal with others. You must learn skills to manage performance and change. You must have the courage to find new ground and establish your authority. In the beginner's mind, there are many possibilities. In the expert's mind, only a few possibilities exist.

> ## The Ham Theory of Inertia
>
> People's easy acceptance of inertia reminds me of the story about the holiday ham.
>
> At a family holiday dinner, the hostess cut off a third of the ham before she placed it in the oven to bake. Her new husband observed this and asked, "Why did you remove part of the ham before baking it?"
>
> His wife replied, "Because that's the way my family has always prepared ham."
>
> Not satisfied with her answer, he approached his young wife's mother and asked: "What's the secret behind cutting off the end of the ham before you bake it?"
>
> His mother-in-law shook her head and replied, "I don't know. That's how my mother did it. Why don't you ask her?"
>
> Still curious, the husband turned to his wife's grandmother and repeated the question. She responded, "That's they way my mother did it. Back then, the hams were too big to fit in our oven."

Remember that first date? Both of you were a little unsure of each other. You wanted a public place, something to entertain you or keep you focused on the event, rather than on each other. Then you had a second date and soon you had an open dialogue of what each of you wanted. The event became less important than being together. The mishaps were less disruptive. The communication, hopefully, was better. You helped each other to understand your needs and wants. You worked together to have fun and enjoy each other. If not, you parted company.

Once attained, you can then help to lead others and help them be responsible for their own changes, just as Bob Greene was a catalyst for Oprah Winfrey. Remember, though, people only decide to change when they decide to change themselves.

As the change takes place, there are two concerns: the actual change and the perceived change. Remember the previous story about the tie? Once I explained to my mother that the first tie I tried on went with my outfit, she saw the outfit as a combination, rather than as separate pieces of clothing. My explanation worked for my mother. A change took place in her. A shift in her thinking was developed. I helped her to see it my way. I didn't argue. I only augmented the obvious to me, which then became obvious to her. Once my mother embraced my concept, her thinking shifted.

Only then does Shift Happen! Only then can you see that adjustments, no matter how minor, can make the system work for your mutual benefit.

According to Jim:
I want everyone to always try to go the extra mile in encouraging thorough, complete, and effective communication.

Attract

7) Mistakes should be viewed as learning opportunities.

Creating an environment in which people feel it's okay to change is important. If employees aren't allowed any creativity or imagination, or if they are denied training, they have less incentive to change. Your job can be made that much more difficult. Customers feel it's their right to be right.

One change impacting companies in all sectors is the level of satisfaction expected by today's consumers. Customers are more aware, more sophisticated, more assertive, and more discerning than they've ever been.

Companies that don't see the marketplace from their Customers' point-of-view run the risk of losing those Customers to their competitors who do. When this happens, companies aren't only losing revenues, they're also incurring costs to attract new Customers. That price is high: it costs 91 percent more to attract a new Customer than to retain an existing one! Put another way, repeat business creates higher profit margins.

"Imagine you are John Akers, CEO of IBM in 1990. In the previous decade, your company had average profits of between $8 billion and $9 billion per year. In 1990, IBM made between $10 billion and $11 billion. No company had ever made that kind of money. You run the most profitable company in the world and have the best-known brand name in the world. The brightest young people in the world at the best universities are asked where they would most like to work and your company is number one.

"God comes to you, John Akers, much as he did to Moses. 'Come up the mountain, John. I want to show you the Promised Land. The era of the mainframe is over. The personal computer is here. If you don't do something dramatic to restructure IBM in 1991, your profits will be zero, and then after that, minus $9 billion, and then the year after that, another minus $9 billion, and the year after that, minus $5 billion. In the next four years, your company is going to lose more than $23 billion—more money than any company in human history. Now, John, it is your job to go down the mountain and persuade 420,000 employees who have had the best decade and the best single year in human history that they have to rip it up and do something different.'

"While a few will fall off a cliff as IBM did, every business is going to have an IBM experience. They will have to change."

—Lester C. Thurow, economist and author of
Building Wealth: The New Rules for Individuals, Companies, and Nations in a Knowledge-Based Economy

According to Jim:
This example won't resonate with many of my readers because no one talks about IBM today. They have fallen so far off the radar that many think IBM is a bodily function children recite when they're young.

Appropriate

8) Your goal is to create long-lasting relationships with Customers.

The wise company focuses on bringing the Customer back. When faced with business decisions, the question becomes not "What do I think is good for the company?" but, rather, "How will this be perceived by our Customers?" The main task is to bring Customers back again and again, and to have them refer new Customers. This only happens if your company is Customer-driven (you'll learn what that is in the following section).

Did you go on the first date without wondering if you would have a second date? Were you genuinely interested in the prospect of getting to know the other person? Once you've made an investment, you expect it to pay off. The same is true with Customers. Customers gave you money and now they want to attain the benefits they expect. As someone once said, "Life is too short not to do it right."

Absolve

9) *Customer-driven* means you're committed to narrowing your knowledge gaps about your Customers.

Companies that are Customer-driven realize if they don't run their businesses to suit their Customers, their Customers will suit themselves—elsewhere. Customers have too many choices today. They don't need you. They can find an alternative solution. If you want to keep your Customers, remember People Express Airlines, Braniff, Atari, Iridium Satellite Phone, and FedEx Fax Service all forgot that people get mad and they just won't take it anymore.

Attention

10) The most important skill you can develop in the pursuit of Customer Satisfaction is listening.

The importance of listening is why God gave us two ears and only one mouth. Customers who complain are Customers who are (or they wouldn't bother complaining!) still interested in doing business with you.

> Blockbuster, the video retail chain survived the transition from VHS to DVD, but then failed to adapt to the changing needs of their renters. Blockbuster remained flatfooted when Netflix starting sending videos in the mail, cable and phone companies started to offer video-on-demand, and Redbox starting using vending machines that rented videos at $1 per night. Blockbuster closed hundreds of stores, attempted to work off their debt and tried to copy some of their competitors.
>
> If Blockbuster had listened to their Customers, they could have had a fighting chance to catch up. But, now, Blockbuster is chasing the industry instead of being the market leader. Listen to your Customers. They'll tell you what they want, need, value, and expect. Simply ask them.

Awareness

11) The Customer-driven company views complaints as opportunities.

Complaints are an opportunity for calculable market research. Complaints are an opportunity to discover problems and remedy them before they become damaging.

Ascertain

12) Complaints are an opportunity to interface with the Customer and improve your relationship.

In short, how your company handles complaints could make the difference between a satisfied and an unsatisfied Customer, with far-reaching consequences. The difference between cats and dogs is this: dogs come when they're called. Cats take a message and get back to you . . . sometimes. Which best describes your company?

Attrition

13) Settle the complaint quickly.

Remember the one bad apple that ruined all the good apples in the barrel? Well, Customers are just like apples. If five dissatisfied Customers complain to thirty people about a negative experience with your company, this means 150 existing or prospective Customers have been put at risk. And it would then take 150 satisfied Customers telling one person how wonderful their experience was to neutralize that impact! As any media watcher knows, bad news is far more sensational and intriguing than good news. This reality underscores why your company has a problem if your Customer has a problem—and why settling problems quickly and positively is so critical.

"Predicting the rain isn't what counts. Building the ark does."
—Unknown

Authorize

14) Give authorization to your staff to settle complaints.

Another effective way to achieve Customer satisfaction is to bring the Customer into the center of the organization. This is the premise of Richard Whiteley and Diane Hessan, authors of the book, *Customer-centered Growth: Five Proven Strategies for Building Competitive Advantage.* They contend that Customer-centered companies have satisfied employees who focus attentively and exclusively on the long-term relationship with the Customer. The bottom line is secondary. Their recommendations:

- Focus like a laser beam on a specific group for whom you create top-of-the-line products or Services.
- Make sure each employee and manager can hear and respond to the voice of the Customer.
- Have every employee engage in the process of collaboration on behalf of the Customer.
- Create hands-on contact leaders who inspire and mobilize employees to provide quality Service to their Customers.

How you handle the complaint should be singularly yours. Empower your staff to deal directly with the Customer.

The following quote can be easily applied to any Customer Service question.

> **"You are responsible for the world you live in. It is not the government's responsibility. It is not your school's or your social club's or your church's or your neighbors' or your fellow citizens'. It is yours, utterly and singularly yours."**
>
> —August Wilson, playwright

The Value of Loyal Customers

The average company today loses half its Customers in five years. You can't grow when Customers are defecting out the back door faster than the sales force can pull new ones in the front door. A 5 percent point increase in Customer Retention in a typical company increases profits by more than 25 percent and increases growth by more than 100 percent! Most companies are feeling the dark side of these loyalty economics today. That is, their profits and growth are being devastated by declining Customer Retention.

How Do You Become Customer-Driven?

Being Customer-driven is easier when the "center of gravity" of your business is kept as close as possible to the point where the action is—the place where the business meets its Customers. Here's how to become Customer-driven:

- Be your own Customer on a regular basis.
- Ask your Customers what they want.
- Listen to those on the front lines.
- Experience your company from the Customer's perspective.
- See your Customers as individual people with needs, wants, and feelings.
- Experience the marketplace firsthand.

> If we are not **Customer Driven...** Our cars won't be either.
>
> Henry Ford

James Feldman

Amazing Examples

Lexus Amazes Customers

In the 100-year-old automobile industry, Customers have rarely been in the driver's seat when it came to purchasing a car at their local dealership. Traditionally, Customers found themselves at the mercy of smooth-talking, highly polished salespeople, armed with arsenals of special deals, closeouts, and demos. This was the case until Lexus revolutionized the sales process and gained legions of enthusiastic fans in the process.

> "The game of business is very much like the game of tennis. Those who fail to master the basics of serving well, usually lose."
>
> —Unknown

What was the secret weapon of Lexus? It simply started over. Without any preconceived notions, Lexus developed a new way of dealing with car buyers that was so distinctive and superior, it flabbergasted Customers.

That new way of dealing with car buyers was treating the Customer with respect. Sales personnel were trained to treat their Customers as their Customers wanted to be treated—as intelligent consumers looking for a car that best met their needs. Even their titles reflect this philosophy—Customers are referred to as "guests" and salespeople are referred to as "consultants." Guests aren't sold; they're "educated" about the benefits derived from owning a Lexus. The company's approach is exemplified by its motto: The relentless pursuit of perfection.

In less than five years, Lexus has positioned itself at the top of the luxury car market. It has stayed there because of the support and loyalty of its Customers. The company has become known for its near-perfect products and landmark Customer interaction process, described by many as "the ultimate Customer-satisfaction experience." Efficient and reliable communication links connecting employees at all levels characterize the corporate culture.

To talk to Lexus owners is to hear them speak of their cars as a valued and beloved family member. While other companies, such as Saturn, have been able to encourage Customer enthusiasm, Lexus has maintained high levels of Customer amazement through its quality product and continual process of refinement in the pursuit of perfection.

The Value of Knowing Your Customers

Lexus paid attention to its Customers. The company realized that less than 15 percent of contemporary households were a traditional nuclear family. It understood people are value-oriented and that today's key values are quality, education, entertainment, and time.

Lexus also recognized that women, as wage earners in dual-income families, are, in many cases, the decision-makers even for purchase decisions such as cars, historically dominated by males.

This realization was incorporated in the guest interaction process. Consultants were trained to present the Lexus story to those who affect decisions. They targeted each member of the family as opposed to the traditional male buyer. To complete the Customer amazement circles, the interaction process involved not only the sales force, but also those behind the front lines.

Apple Introduced Friendly Computers

As Customers become more sophisticated, they no longer merely buy a product. Customers buy the benefits they get from using the product. Apple computers are a case-in-point. People who own Apple computers exhibit a loyalty that is extraordinary, especially in an industry known for planned obsolescence. Even with Apple's current difficulties, its Customers hang on, hoping their beloved computers will once again emerge at the forefront of technology. Apple introduced the iPhone, iPad, MacBook Air, and iTunes, which weren't replacements for its existing products, but a new entry to new Customers. Apple was clever in identifying its new Customer as one who wanted easy use for a smartphone, light-weight tablets and computers, and the ability to download one song at a time. No skills were needed and it was simple to send email, surf, and order online. Successful? Greater profits? New Customers? Higher profit margins? Apple did what many companies have tried and failed. Apple reinvented itself time and time again. And Apple continues to bring us user-friendly products. Now the PC environment, Android, and others have realized that it's the "product of the product" that people purchase. Make it simple. Make it useful. Make it affordable. Make it for the masses and the masses will buy it.

> "God himself could not sink this ship."
> —Thomas Andrews, principal architect for the RMS Titanic

User-Oriented Design

Apple Customers have the relationship they do now because, early on, Apple offered them a hassle-free, reliable way to enter the technological age. With Apple, they didn't have to worry about whether the lighting was right or to remember what keyboard configuration or interface went with what software. Apple's user-friendly design took the intimidation out of computing and made it fast, easy, and fun. Until the departure of John Sculley III, a passionate connectedness existed between Apple and its Customers—so much so that Customers were probably the greatest sales force the company had. Management focused on its employees, promoted talent, and encouraged the individual mind to create within the collective spirit. Input was sought from Customers, distributors, engineers, software writers—virtually anyone who could help improve the way the products were manufactured and Serviced.

This contributed greatly to the high-level of Customer Satisfaction experienced in an industry where technological failures and Customer frustration were all too common.

New Leaders

In Customer-centered companies, such as Lexus and Apple, the old models of leadership are gone, including sitting back, giving directions, and having everyone else do the work.

The Customer-oriented leader comes in regular contact with their center of gravity, where the Customer buys or uses the product or Service being sold. The net result is these companies get employees and end users excited about their products or Services, and confident in the companies' capabilities to perform beyond expectations. Now they produce new products geared to new Customers.

They abandoned their old Customers by creating products for the Internet and non-Internet-savvy Customers. Plug into the phone line, plug into the wall, and you're ready to surf. What did these companies do to the older Customers? They made their equipment totally obsolete.

They changed their connections, changed their operating system, and took away any accessible technical support.

Unfortunately, for many years, Apple lost sight of its business Customer. The company was almost practically nonexistent in the business sector. On the other hand, Apple found new Customers and turned the company around.

Today, Apple spends as much time on the business consumer as the personal user. This is a great example of realizing that changing your Customer focus can result in finding new Customers who embrace your products or Services. Apple doesn't care about the old Customers . . . in fact, it abandoned them. Apple found enough new Customers to revive the company's sagging bottom line.

Jobs vs. Cook

If your question is, "Which CEO is better, Jobs or Cook?" Jobs was the perfect leader for Apple when it was struggling back to the top in the 1990s, and to make it a world-beating giant this century. Jobs was a visionary, with a remarkable ability to gauge the consumer market. Under his tenure, Apple released numerous iconic products like the Mac, the iPod, the iPhone, and the iPad that made what Apple is today. Cook is perhaps a better "peacetime" general, though. Cook took over a company valued at $347 billion in 2011. Under his steady hand, Apple hit $922 billion in 2018. He's also driven Apple to become a 100 percent sustainable energy-powered company. Thanks to Cook's operational wizardry, Apple benefits from an amazing supply chain, an enormous network of Apple Store distribution centers, and the ability to control almost every element of its narrative.

Compare that to Zappos or Hyundai. They have leaders, but it's the company culture, not one person, that resonates with their Customers. Their Service mantra is simple: if their Customer has a problem, the company has a problem, so they try to settle the Customer complaint quickly.

> "Remember, the sixties happened in the early seventies, and that's when I came of age; and to me, the spark of that was there was something *beyond* what you see every day."
>
> —Steve Jobs, *Steve Jobs: The Lost Interview*

According to Jim:

The two primary ingredients of growth are personal VALUE and SUSTAINABLE opportunity. Make informed choices.

In contrast, Lexus continually tries to improve its relationship with existing Customers. The result? Lexus has successfully introduced additional models into the marketplace and the company enjoys the highest resale value on preowned models. Yet, as you look at their competition, Lexus faces new rivals, such as Hyundai, Kia, Nissan, BMW, and others that have also reinvented themselves. No longer is the nameplate recognition as important as the value and comfort that promises safety, technology, and a Customer-centered dealer/Service network. Shift Happens!® and the car companies are now driven to reach their Customers.

Nordstrom Department Store

Who can profile Customer-centered companies without acknowledging Nordstrom, a retailer that has become a national model for outstanding Customer Service? This family-run business includes its Customers as extended family and communicates with them one-to-one. In his book, *The Nordstrom Way,* Robert Spector proposes three keys to Nordstrom's success:

Key #1: The first key revolves around the merchandise. Buyers work closely with manufacturers to obtain the best selection, value, and quality of goods. Salespeople are expected to have a complete understanding of the merchandise and its features.

Key #2: The second key is the workforce. Nordstrom would rather hire nice people and teach them to sell than to hire experienced salespeople and teach them to be nice! Through extraordinary rates of expansion, Nordstrom has created a fast Service track for energetic, highly entrepreneurial people who are rewarded for their performance through sales commissions.

Store managers have the freedom to hire a huge sales staff and they are responsible for training, coaching, nurturing, and evaluating their sales teams. Buying is decentralized: managers are encouraged to buy as much inventory as their shelves can hold, and to solicit input on fashion direction, styles, colors, quantities, and sizes—because they know best what the Customer wants. Decisions get made closest to the point of sale, the business's center of gravity.

Key #3: The third key to Nordstrom's success is its total emphasis on the Customer. Nordstrom believes in creating a memorable experience for its Customers. To do this, Nordstrom's features more seating, larger fitting rooms, and wider aisles than its competitors.

A tuxedo-clad pianist plays live music. In the shoe department, the chairs have arms and taller legs, so Customers can concentrate on buying shoes, rather than on how to get out of the chair gracefully. It's this level of detail that earns Customer accolades.

Create Legends

Employees are instructed always to make decisions in favor of the Customer over the company. The store's primary rule is to use your good judgment in all situations. Salespeople are never criticized for doing too much for the Customer, only for doing too little.

Nowhere is this more evident than in "Heroics," true tales of incredible Customer Service that is part and parcel of the Nordstrom corporate culture and mythology.

Nordstrom: Tales of Incredible Customer Service

A Customer, who was on her way to catch a flight at Sea-Tac Airport in Seattle, inadvertently left her airline ticket on a counter in Nordstrom's women's apparel department. Discovering the ticket, her sales associate immediately phoned the airline and asked the representative if he could track down the Customer at the airport and write another ticket. The answer was "No." (That airline should take lessons from Nordstrom!) Not having enough time to get her car out of the garage, the Nordstrom salesperson jumped into a cab, rode out to the airport, located the Customer, and delivered the ticket herself in time for the woman to make her flight.

A woman purchased a pair of jeans at Nordstrom and was advised by the sales associate to wear them, wash them multiple times, and then bring them back to be shortened, free of charge. Following this advice, the Customer returned and the alteration person pinned the hem. The Customer returned to pick up the jeans a week later, but she didn't have time to try them on. At home, when the Customer took the jeans out of the bag, she discovered they had never been altered! The Customer went back to the store and explained what had happened to the senior salesperson in the department. With abject embarrassment, the salesperson apologized and promised the jeans would be fixed by that same afternoon. When the Customer said she couldn't return then, the salesperson offered to drive the jeans to her home when she finished her shift. The salesperson said she would stay to make sure the jeans fit correctly. And the salesperson was as good as her word.

Love can be difficult, love can be costly, and love can be perplexing. You can be disappointed in love many times before you find the real thing. But, when you do find love, it changes your life and there is never any question that the quest has been worth it. And, when you think about it, don't you find the same is true of a great company delivering great Customer Service?

Ambitious

15) Make sure your Customers are satisfied. Ask them!

Keeping your Customer satisfied is the refrain sung by the leader of a cross section of companies and industries including transportation, technology, communication, manufacturing, and retail. Savvy leaders have learned that keeping Customers means knowing Customers, and knowing Customers means hearing and responding to them. You must be supportive to sustain the relationship.

> "We know exactly where we want to go because our Customers will show us the way."
>
> —Jerre L. Stead, CEO,
> AT&T Global Information Solutions

According to Jim:

It's too bad AT&T has lost Mr. Stead. They no longer listen because they fail to remember they are a communication company.

As an example of a changing program, let's consider improving Customer Service. Your company can sail through the storms of change like a Lexus or a Nordstrom if you have the commitment from senior management to create a winning Customer-Service strategy. But without buy-in from the top of the organization, employees are unlikely to champion the program.

Just how do you go about creating such a program? Like any change, step-by-step. Here are ten suggestions recommended by the Organizational Development Corporation in its "Redesigning Customer Care" newsletter for creating a winning Customer Care strategy in your company.

> I. **Establish Creditability.** One of the best ways to communicate a new mandate effectively is to create a team whose members represent as many functional areas as possible and to have company clout in the eyes of employees. Without this authority, roadblocks could develop because other departments, managers, and frontline staff don't view the team as having the authority to make them change. Employees must understand this change is supported throughout the organization, has full commitment from the top, and involves them. The team must effectively communicate to employees and generate enthusiasm.

"When the window of opportunity appears, do not pull down the shade."

—Thomas J. ("Tom") Peters,
American business writer, speaker, and consultant

Only when the program is fully championed does it have any hope of succeeding. To receive adequate attention, substantial priority and time must be devoted to the program.

> II. **Prioritize Customer Service Issues.** One of the first tasks of the team is to identify—objectively and quantitatively—the issues that have the greatest impact on Customer Service. One effective method is to survey Customers, either through anonymous questionnaires or focus groups. Also useful is to survey Customers who have defected to determine why they went elsewhere.

Another source of information is feedback centers (Customer complaint areas, information desks, receptionists, sales staff, and so forth). Once the information is collected, rank the responses numerically and according to revenue loss. This can help the team focus on solutions that can save or generate the most dollars for the program.

I have spent the better part of my life observing people. I make notes to myself, which I later incorporate into my presentations, blogs, and virtual presentations to come up with tools, structures, and processes. That same principle can be applied to Customer Service performance. For any system to work, the efforts, successes, and failures need to be documented and shared. To create a Customer-centric organization, each person who interacts with a Customer should be able to take the broad swaths of wisdom, and then reduce them to simple, practical tools, which allow the entire organization to apply those principles.

Review Customer Feedback at Three Levels

Before you collect Customer data, you should have a plan to use it. A top executive group should use the results to allocate resources and decide on direction. Middle management groups should use the data to help support line functions. Groups of line people should look at the findings and report back up the hierarchy on what they need to improve performance. Big data is hard to filter. Unlike the VP of Customer Experience at a very large company who never leaves his desk to visit a Customer or makes a personal attempt to find out what the Customer values, make sure you have a plan.

> III. **Establish Realistic Goals.** After identifying the key Customer Service issues, it's time to agree on which problems to solve first and to set target completion dates. Issues can be ranked again—this time according to the level of activity required to solve them.

Attaching time lines to each issue is also necessary to track results. The *A* list might require multiple levels of approval, involve major technical support, take six months or more, and so forth. The *B* list might require input from other departments, but it might not require significant paperwork or investment. The *C* list might require minimal activity, such as changing staff coverage or reinforcing a policy that has fallen through the cracks. This is often a good place to start because you can demonstrate immediate results and get staff to "buy into" the program.

> "The world has just changed so radically, and we're all running to catch up."
>
> —Sam Neill, *Jurassic Park*

IV. Endorse the Program. Once the team is clear about its goals and time line, it's time to kickoff the program at the corporate or department level. This is the time to introduce the team, share the vision, and communicate the intentions of the program and level of involvement.

> "We do not come to work in the morning and think about how we can do against GM or Toyota. We think the way to win is to focus on the Customer."
>
> —Alexander J. Trotman, former head of Worldwide Operations, Ford Motor Company

V. Raise Staff Awareness. Meet with staff on a smaller scale and educate them as to what quality Service means to your company. Your staff can do many exercises to become more Customer-oriented—from identifying all internal and external Customers to creating its top ten tips to improve Customer Service.

VI. Implement Continuous Quality Improvement Circles. Input from frontline staff is critical to the successes of a winning Customer Service strategy. To encourage participation, create employee-centered, continuous improvement (quality groups that address the Customer, employee performance levels, and work processes).

VII. Develop Product and Service Quality Standards. Staff and management together should establish standards of excellence, followed by key performance indicators for employees. In this way, employees know what's expected of them on a daily, weekly, and monthly basis, as well as what's considered "excelling." Many supervisors find negotiation with staff results in higher productivity and levels of commitment to Service.

VIII. Benchmark. Keeping score of performance levels and achievements by tracking key results on a company-wide level is important. You can establish several months of results so performance comparisons can be made, either by time or by group. One positive benefit of benchmarking is many individuals begin to improve their performance levels when they know they're being tracked. Publicizing results on a regular basis to keep the momentum going is important.

Make Benchmarking Fun

When you hear about a great idea another business is using, send out an "exploration party." Make it fun. For example, use the company van and rush everyone to the scene of good Customer Service. Encourage people to take notes and actually apply the lessons when they get back to the office or store. Invite employees to report good business experiences to their supervisors, so your company can benefit. It's informal benchmarking, and it's a way to get everyone involved in continuous improvement.

> IX. **Recognize and Reward.** Initiating an employee incentive program can recognize, reinforce, and reward top performers, as well as remind staff of the importance of their jobs and the company's goals.

"In the long run, our Customers are going to determine whether we have a job. Their attitude toward us is going to be the factor determining our success. Every employee must resolve that their most important duty is our Customers."
—Joseph C. Wilson, IV, Xerox CEO, 1961–67

One reward is the bonus incentive, which attaches dollar amounts to goals achieved. Employees like the bonus incentive because they're rewarded for their hard work and they can earn extra money. Another type of plan is the creative incentive, which can take the form of well-timed surprises or individually tailored perks, including free trips, days off, and so forth. A third recognition program is the Employee of the Month award, which creates competition and public acknowledgment of individual achievements. If you take good care of your employees, they'll take good care of your Customers.

> X. **Promote Your Company's Quality Customer Service.** Once your company can consistently reach the Service and quality goals that are established, and you can be certain you have a

proven track record, it's time to blow your horn a little. Publicity can be created through paid advertising, a direct mail program to Customers, in-house visuals (T-shirts, banners, posters, billboards, mugs, and so forth), and sales collateral. A catchy slogan (perhaps derived through an employee contest) can be part of a publicity campaign.

At this point, you might think you've finished what you set out to do, but few companies ever reach the ultimate stage of Customer Satisfaction. Why? Because many variables are constantly changing. This makes creating and maintaining a Customer-driven organization an ongoing process.

"You celebrate the victory, but you analyze the defeat."
—Bill Walton, former pro basketball star

Remember the watch company from the previous chapter?

Once we learned the management didn't understand its role in providing Customer Service, seeing how the company fell short of reasonable expectations for communication, fulfillment, and understanding of the situation was easy. The company assumed a refund would make everything okay, but what was needed was a solution. After all, the Customer had a need and the refund didn't satisfy that need.

"I solemnly promise and declare that for every Customer who comes within ten feet of me, I will smile, look them in the eye, and greet them, so help me Sam."
—Employee pledge, Wal-Mart Stores, Inc.

If you stay focused on your Customer and keep improving how you care for them, however, you'll realize significant results. This kind of focus can never stop, just as in dating, courtship, and marriage. You must always dazzle your date, anticipating their needs and wants. And you must always treat your Customer or your date as they expect to be treated.

Action Summary

Change is an inexorable fact of life. How you react to change is up to you. Positive or negative, Shift Happens!® and Customer Service demands you respond to those changes. Here are 12 actionable ways to help you navigate the seas of Customer Service demands:

1. Walk the talk. If you want others to bring about Customer Service change, be willing to take the lead.
2. Continually increase the number of people taking responsibility for their own changes.
3. Embrace improvisations as the best path for better performance and change.
4. Encourage lateral thinking, creativity, and imagination.
5. Use team performance to drive change.
6. Concentrate organizational designs on the work people do, rather than on the decision-making authority they have.
7. Sell ideas by sharing results. Make everyone a part of the solution. Include the results in your social media marketing. Tweet, Facebook, LinkedIn, and YouTube all provide an opportunity to show the results to your Customers.
8. Put people in the position to learn by doing. Provide the information and support they need in time to perform.
9. Treat mistakes as learning moments. Aim for success, not perfection.
10. Confront your fears and allow yourself to be human.
11. Asking dumb questions is easier than correcting dumb mistakes.
12. Do unto your Customer as you would like to have done for you.

Remember, D ♥ A ♥ T ♥ I ♥ N ♥ G Is Fun!

15 Ideas to Anticipate

1. Don't resist the idea of change—or the implementation of change.
2. Embrace change and manage it the best way you can.
3. View change as a process.
4. View the process of change as a moving target.
5. Your Customers *always* think they are right.
6. Managing during periods of change often requires changing yourself.
7. Mistakes should be viewed as learning opportunities.
8. Your goal is to create long-lasting relationships with your Customers.
9. Customer-driven means you're committed to narrowing your knowledge gaps about your Customers.
10. The most important skill you can develop in the pursuit of Customer Satisfaction is listening. The Customer-driven company views complaints as opportunities.
11. Complaints are an opportunity to interface with the Customer and improve your relationship.
12. Settle the complaint quickly.
13. Give authorization to your staff to settle complaints.
14. Make sure your Customers are satisfied. Ask them!
15. Replicate what works. Replace what doesn't. And that includes your suppliers, associates, and management.

According to Jim:

The principles of D ʘ A ʘ T ʘ I ʘ N ʘ G are like mirrors you can use to reflect great Customer Service.

James Feldman

T Is for TREAT
21 Thoughtful Ways to Keep Your Customers Returning to Do Business with Your Company

Treat

1) **To ensure a long-term, beneficial relationship, handle your clients respectfully, individually, and attentively.**

   "Treat your Customers as an appreciating asset."
   —Thomas J. ("Tom") Peters,
   American business writer, speaker, and consultant

   A profitable business starts and ends with the Customer. By placing the Customer at the center of all your thinking, you create an environment that fosters long-term success. You hear about certain companies that treat their Customers with superior Service and others that ignore them.

   A key component of success lies in your company's capability to generate repeat and referral business. A sure way to do this is by forming lasting relationships with your Customers.

Your Customers are not concerned with Yesterday.

It's what you did for them today that really matters.

Training

2) Excellent Customer Service must be cultivated through ongoing proper guidance and flawless coordination of people and procedures.

Thinking great Customer Service is something that just happens is foolish. Great Customer Service requires constant training. Customers often teach suppliers how they want to be treated. Certainly, the Internet has given a voice to Customers, which enables them to voice their opinions—good or bad—to millions of readers.

Training is a three-part process:

The first part of training is the external Customer, the person who is making the purchase.

The external Customer makes the purchase because that Customer believes the product or Service can provide a solution to a problem. Think about this for a moment. What was the last purchase you made that wasn't used to solve a problem? You purchased food because you were hungry. You went to a movie to be entertained. You bought a new tie, so you could look good at a job interview or special event. Cable television solved your problem of what to do or what to watch, when you have the time. Purchases are made for a reason and, if that reason can be satisfied with a particular product or Service, then you made a good purchase. If you find your needs aren't being satisfied, then the problem isn't solved and a new one is created: returning or canceling the purchase.

The second part of training is the internal Customer. This is the team that makes up every part of the company—from production to fulfillment, from billing to returns—everyone in the company must embrace the concept of exceeding Customer expectations. Like dating someone from a large family, or even a small one, you need the approval of everyone to make sure your concentrated efforts aren't diluted by others.

"Leaders are people who do the right things. Managers are people who do things right. There is a profound difference. When you think about the right things, your mind immediately goes toward thinking about the future, thinking about dreams, missions, visions, strategic intent, purpose. But when you think about doing things right, you think about control mechanisms. You think about how-to. Leaders ask the what and why questions, not the how questions. Leaders think about empowerment, not control. And the best definition of empowerment is that you don't steal responsibility from your people."
—Warren G. Bennis, leadership guru and professor, University of Southern California

The third part of training is creating an integration of procedures that works well for both internal and external Customers. Employee empowerment is the key. If the first person who hears a complaint is empowered to handle the complaint, the issue gets resolved quickly. If the first person has to talk to another person, the size of the problem, in the opinion of the Customer, has just doubled.

According to Jim:
Imagine everyone has a sign around their neck that reads, WIIFM (What's in it for me?). Make them all feel important.

Each person in the organization must realize their contribution is as important as anyone else's. Teams aren't built around one person. Just like a date, each one builds on the previous encounter. You start to have a history. You understand the needs and wants of your date, and you try to make sure their goals are reached before yours. To be successful on a date (or in business), you need a mission and the dedication to make that mission a reality. No matter what your mission, you must have the single-minded focus to reach that goal. Otherwise, you're simply wasting time.

> "A jet aircraft has a lot of different parts, like the wings, a cockpit, and a fuselage. The components all look different, use different materials, and require different levels of precision in their workmanship. Each performs a different function but, as a whole, they have a single purpose: to fly."
>
> —Teichi Sakaiya, author of *What Is Japan?*

According to Jim:

Organizations need to heighten the awareness of their tremendous need for dedication to Customer Satisfaction.

What about your organization? Does it have lots of parts that don't function well as a whole?

Timeliness

3) Set up your Service to deliver answers and solutions when the Customer needs it. That means NOW!

In the world of the fast-paced Internet, Customer Service has become the main reason people do business with one firm or another. Recently, I made a purchase on the Internet from Balducci's, a gourmet food supplier. The package arrived in great condition, shrink-wrapped, with instructions to place the food in the freezer.

Following the instructions, I immediately placed the items in the freezer. Several weeks passed before I found time to prepare some of the food. After I opened the meat products, I found instructions that included a reference to the marinade recipe, the gravy recipe, and the easy side dishes. I searched everywhere and found nothing.

After I tried to reach Customer Service by phone, I sent them an email memo. The phone lines were still busy and, after waiting ten minutes, I decided to send an email, per the instructions on the site.

In my email, I indicated the date was Friday, December 15, 2:30 P.M. CST and my plan was to prepare the meal on Saturday, December 16. I asked for copies of the recipes, which weren't included in my package. On Monday, December 18 at 9:10 P.M., I received the following reply.

> Thank you for contacting Balducci's.com. A member of our consumer support team will respond to your message within one business day. Internet Customer Service
>
> balduccis.com
>
> http://www.balduccis.com
>
> **This is an automatic message. A reply to this message will not be seen by your consumer specialist.

Not only was this message useless, it was untimely as well. While I understand the Customer Service department might be going home for the weekend on Friday afternoon, I didn't understand an auto-response message coming 72 hours later to tell me it would be yet another day before a response would be provided. Balducci's is a very expensive, high-quality food purveyor, which, obviously, doesn't understand the need for timely Customer Service.

How can any company that provides gourmet food products not have Customer Service on the weekend? Isn't it reasonable to expect that most gourmet meals would be served then? Certainly, an auto-response could be set to activate with messages that include 800 numbers or other assistance if the Customer Service department is closed. Timeliness, tact, and training are all needed.

If you're going to provide Service to your Customers, you must make sure the Service provided is timely. Yesterday's newspaper is full of news that was important the day it was printed but, otherwise, it's almost worthless, except to a person who just came off an undersea adventure or a climb to the Himalayas, where newspapers are scarce.

According to Jim:

Time is the only inventory we can't replace. Create a need so strong that clients say, "I need you, I need your products, and I need your Services."

Teamwork

4) Realize that it takes everyone involved to consistently produce superior Customer Service.

Composer-performer Lionel Richie wrote and organized the production of the popular song "We Are The World." Richie invited the luminaries of the music world to collaborate on the record to raise money for the starving in Africa. On the day of the recording, Richie posted a sign next to the studio entrance that said, "Check your ego at the door." His message was clear. The success of the record depended on everyone working together.

5) In the simplest of terms, working together means great Customer Service.

Instead of pointing fingers, everyone in the organization has one goal: to exceed Customer expectations. Later in this chapter, you'll see three examples of how various teams functioned in trying to reach that simple goal. Whether the Customer is right or wrong isn't the point; it's a matter of whether you want to keep the Customer coming back.

> "Crew is the ultimate team sport. A member of a crew has a definite individual job to do. But the crew wins or loses as a team. A winning boat has every rower pulling together ... and it doesn't carry anybody who is just along for the ride."
>
> —J. Lawrence ("Larry") Wilson, CEO of Rohm and Hass, on the value of teamwork

6) Look for examples of teams that function well together.

For six seasons, the Chicago Bulls were unstoppable. With Michael Jordan, they won six championships, but it wasn't six in a row. To the contrary, Jordan left to try his skills at baseball. While Jordan was gone, the team didn't win the championship—not once. Once Jordan returned, though, he once again became the catalyst to make the Chicago Bulls unbullievable.

Find your team captain and create a winning team by understanding Customers aren't satisfied by one person or one department. Customer

Service isn't a department; Customer Service is an attitude. A group becomes a team when all members are sure enough of themselves and their contributions to praise the skills of others.

> **"When I ran training seminars for new employees at American Airlines, I kept returning to this truth. I'd explain to the agents in my group that every day, thousands of employees worked incredibly hard to ensure a passenger's loyalty to American Airlines. But if a reservation was wrong, or the ticket was written incorrectly, or the flight got out late, or the crew was unfriendly, or the bag was missing, it didn't matter to the passenger that everything else was perfect. One mistake by one employee could mean that the work of thousands—from the corporate office to the maintenance hanger to the cockpit crew—had gone for naught."**
> —John M. Capozzi, President, JMC Industries, 1994

Rick Majerus, head coach of the University of Utah basketball team, said of his team's success in the Final Four, "We break every huddle with the cry of 'TEAM.' We play it, we yell it, we believe it."

Each person on the team contributes like a spoke of a wheel. When one spoke is broken, the others have to work harder, if possible, to make the wheel stay on track. Sooner or later, the wheel can't function any longer and all motion stops. The same is true for any organization.

I remember purchasing a Canon copier. The salesman told me the model I bought was the best, the fastest, and the most economical copier in the marketplace. He left it for our office to try for a few weeks. It performed as promised. We copied on two sides, we collated, we stapled, and we applauded the way it made our copy needs seem like a simple child's game. Place in the original, push a few buttons, and, like magic, the work was done.

I eagerly purchased this "wiz-bang" copier for our office. Within two days, the copier jammed and we called for Service. It took four phone calls and two days before the technician arrived. He opened the copier and spilled toner all over the floor. Because our office was in a loft building with hardwood floors, this was easy to clean up.

What we didn't realize at the time was the toner was leaking through the cracks in the floor to the office beneath us. Papers were ruined, clothes were soiled, and that office had a terrible mess to clean.

During the tirade that followed from the office below, the technician informed us that additional parts had to be ordered. He also told us that because of his schedule, he couldn't return for several more days to make the repair. I called the salesman. No return call. I called the sales manager. No return call. Our brand-new copier was a brand-new nightmare. Not only did we have no copier, we also had a very unhappy neighbor. The disruption to the office was magnified when we received an invoice for $3,500 for clean up and replacement of materials in the damaged office. A visit from our landlord informed us that, under the terms of our lease, we were responsible and he demanded a check immediately. When I explained the situation, he showed me the lease, highlighted in yellow where our responsibilities were outlined.

Again I called the salesman. No return call. I called the Service supervisor and asked for expedited Service. He assured me the person doing the repair would try to get there sooner. The Service supervisor did offer an alternative solution, however: another Service person was in the building and he could call to see if anything could be done to resolve the problem.

As soon as the Service technician arrived, he looked at the copier and said, "Oh no, not another one of these pieces of cr_p." When I asked what he meant, the technician said this was the worst performing unit in the line. When it worked, it was great. When it malfunctioned, it was impossible to repair quickly. In fact, he said, it had the highest downtime of all their units.

It took three months, my attorney, and many hours of testimony to get the copier removed, my money refunded, and the out-of-pocket expenses reimbursed. Clearly, if the Service technician and the salesman had been on the same team with the same goals, we could have had a very different experience.

7) Customers expect honesty from everyone on the team.

If one person doesn't live up to expectations, the entire team suffers. Before you make a move, consider how it could affect others. Leaders must adopt a "think for the team" approach to any issue.

TEAM = Together Everyone Achieves More, or as I like to say it:

Talent +

Enthusiasm +

Attitude +

Motivation

Either way, these elements make a winning **TEAM**.

Teach

8) Remember the way to win an argument with a Customer is to begin by being right.

Once you have that foundation, you can explain your viewpoint and, perhaps, only by chance, convince your Customer they were misguided, misunderstood, or totally mistaken. Otherwise, don't bother.

9) Solving a Customer Service issue requires many people skills.

Remember how easily problems used to be solved? The Lone Ranger and his faithful Indian companion Tonto come riding into town. Within minutes, the Lone Ranger understands the problem, identifies the bad guys, and sets out to catch them.

The Lone Ranger draws his gun and quickly outwits the bad guys, but he never seriously injures anyone. Then, he has the bad guys behind bars. And there's that wonderful scene at the end. The now-saved victims stand in front of their ranch or in the town square marveling at how wonderful life is now that they've been saved. You hear hoof beats and "The William Tell Overture." One person turns to another and asks, "Who was that masked man?" The other person replies, "Why, that was the Lone Ranger!" If only life were that easy.

10) It isn't that Customers don't see the solution. It's that they can't see the problem.

Customers today are armed with information about your company, your products and Services, the costs, and the competition. They know they can vote with their dollars and they exercise their right to do just that. By the time Customers come to you with a problem, they have already told others, formulated their defense (or offense) tactic, and planned for their rebuttal.

11) Customers feel the person or company that sold them the product or Service must be responsible for its performance.

And, sometimes, it's impossible to remember difficulties are only made to be overcome. Great Customer Service means you

- Listen well
- Answer cautiously
- Make good use of other people's brains
- Make sure you know more than you're expected to know
- Decide promptly
- Treat failures as stepping stones to further effort
- Master all details
- Never put your hand out further than you can withdraw it

Trust

"Quality Customer Service isn't about money. It's about caring. It's creating a trust between you and your Customer. It's about wanting to be the best, all over the globe. It's an obvious and well-known fact that mountain climbers don't like to buy discounted climbing ropes. And there's the joke about the parachute offer for sale—cheap, slightly irregular, but used only once. When something is as important as life and death—and all business decisions should be—quality is irreplaceable."

—Hap Klopp, President, The North Face,
the world's largest producer of outdoor adventure equipment

12) Quality Customer Service begins with quality products and quality thinking.

We must trust our suppliers, our employees, and our Customers.

If we believe our Customers are trying to take advantage of us, then it becomes difficult to trust their comments or reasons in asking for some adjustment.

Trust is a two-way street
On all coins minted in the US, the inscription "In God We Trust" appears. For all others, trust must be earned. Trust is a continuous, never-ending commitment to improvement.

Problems are simple. Unfortunately, people aren't simple. We can never predict Customers' demands or rationale. We can only make their choice in doing business with us an enjoyable experience. The best preparation for tomorrow's Customer demands is to do today's work superbly well.

"Don't fight the problem. Decide it."

—George C. Marshall, General of the US Army,
the "Organizer of Victory"

Tackle

13) It's important to deal immediately with problems and negative issues while they're fresh and still somewhat small.

By staying in contact with your Customers on a regular basis, you can avoid surprises. You'll be given the opportunity to show you are the consummate professional with extensive product knowledge. And, even more important, you can let each of your Customers know they are the most important Customer you have.

Tackling the problem is something we all hate to do, but if we avoid it or let it fester, a small problem becomes a much bigger one.

> "I hated every minute of training, but I said, 'Don't quit. Suffer now and live the rest of your life as champion.'"
>
> —Muhammad Ali

14) Meet the problem head on, and make sure you and your Customer agree on the solution.

Sometimes, the conversation can reveal more than the demands. Customers are people who simply want to be treated as if they're important to your business . . . and they are.

Stop for a minute and think about all the companies that forgot how important their Customers were to their success.

Eastman Kodak. For nearly a century, no company commercialized the camera as successfully as Kodak, whose breakthroughs included the Brownie camera in 1900, Kodachrome color film, the handheld movie camera, and the easy-load Instamatic camera. Kodak was arrogant with their dealers. It often forced products into the camera store that weren't wanted by the dealer. In its heyday, Kodak controlled the photo products such as film, processing, photographic paper, slide projectors, and more.

But with the advent of digital photography and all the printers, software, file sharing, and third-party apps that Kodak has mostly missed out on, the change from film to digital media dismissed the need for Kodak's most profitable products—film, chemicals, and photo paper—which were needed for conventional "film to paper" photography. Since the late 1980s, Kodak has tried to expand into pharmaceuticals, memory chips, healthcare and health-Service imaging, document management, and many other fields, but the magic never returned. Kodak's stock price is now about 96 percent below the peak it hit in 1997. Today, Kodak is selling off real estate worth more than the patents, products, and processes it once controlled.

Sony. Sony never listened to its Customers. The company was slow moving, but innovative. Just a decade ago, the Walkman was as popular as the iPod. Sony dominated most of the personal consumer electronics, but it lost sight of its Customers by becoming too diversified. Sony lost its leadership because the company failed to develop software rather than hardware. Today, Sony doesn't dominate any product category the way it did before. Samsung, LG, HTC, VIZIO, and, of course, Apple all focus their lens on the consumer, while Sony focuses on film and music divisions, which sell its products through its competitors.

Motorola. Motorola dominated a business that relied on communication, yet it didn't listen. It started its business with car radios, then two-way radios, and then it invented the mobile phone. Yes, Motorola invented cell phones. And it dominated the cell phone business ten years ago. Consumers told Motorola they want the phone to do more, to become smarter, but Motorola didn't listen. Apple, LG, Samsung, and RIM all took so much market share so quickly, Motorola was forced to sell its cell phone division to Google. Listen to your Customers. They will tell you what they'll buy. At this writing, Motorola is on the block. It has sold off many of its divisions and now the corpus may become the corpse.

Apple. When Steve Jobs was alive, Apple was voted the most Innovative Company in the world. After Jobs's death, Apple dropped from being #1 to the Top 10, but no longer #1. However, I must point out, Apple's Customer Service has always ranked in the Top 5 for over two decades. Apple knows the Customer will pay more, return more often, and remain loyal if it provides the Service that's demanded from the Apple Customer. Want an amazing Customer experience? Visit any Apple store. Make a purchase in Boston, and then ask for assistance in San Francisco. Apple will provide first-class Service everywhere, every time.

According to Jim:

Competition demands you stay alert and attuned to your Customer. Shift Happens!® and we all have to deal with it.

Zappos. Zappos is to Internet shoe sales as Amazon is to books. Zappos has created a Customer Service culture that's become legendary. Here is Zappos ten-step Customer Service Culture.

1. Deliver WOW Through Service.
2. Embrace and Drive Change.
3. Create Fun and a Little Weirdness.
4. Be Adventurous, Creative, and Open-Minded.
5. Pursue Growth and Learning.
6. Build Open and Honest Relationships with Communication.
7. Build a Positive Team and Family Spirit.
8. Do More with Less.
9. Be Passionate and Determined.
10. Be Humble.

Thankful

15) Show your Customers you appreciate their business by asking for their feedback, and then listen to them.

Many companies forget the reason they're in business is their Customers. Experience is something you don't get until just after you need it. If this is the case with exceptional Customer Service, however, your business will fail. Find a way to make Customers start thinking about your product or Services. Ask your Customers for their opinions. If you're always thankful for your Customers, even when they complain, you learn more about how to satisfy them. Many great failures in business could have been avoided if Customer input had been part of the on-going implementation plan.

"The boat is unsinkable. I cannot imagine any condition which would cause this ship to flounder. I cannot conceive of any vital disaster happening to this vessel. Modern shipbuilding has gone beyond that."

—Captain E. J. Smith, Vice President of the White Star Line, speaking about its newest ship, the Titanic

According to Jim:

Professionals built the Titanic. Amateurs build the ark.

16) Think about every problem and every challenge you face.

The solution to each problem starts with education. For the sake of the future of your business, you must transform your Customer Service response to reach higher levels. The days of status quo are over. Giants have been toppled by bad Service. Companies that controlled markets have been dissolved by the drip method of one Customer after another leaving.

According to Jim:

Customers pay you to sweat all the details, so it's easy and pleasant for them to use your products and Services.

I remember being in a McDonald's restaurant during a busy lunch hour. A youngster was waiting in line with a dollar in his hand. As the child approached the sales counter, the clerk didn't see him and waited on the much taller adult behind the boy. This was repeated several times as the child waited patiently.

The manager of the store was restocking the paper products when he saw what was happening. He rushed over to the counter and knelt down beside the child and apologized. The manager asked the child what he wanted, took the order, and gave him the large fries. When the child handed him the money, the manager said, "No, Sir. I'm very sorry you had to wait. This is on us!"

The child turned around with a radiant smile and proclaimed to the entire store: "He called me 'Sir!' He said 'I'm sorry' . . . WOW!" The entire restaurant burst into applause. We all learned something about Customer Service that day and how to exceed *any* Customer's expectations. Every adult needs a child to teach them: it's the way adults learn.

I wrote a letter to McDonald's headquarters about this remarkable event. Less than a week later, I received a call from the store manager thanking me. Confused, I asked how he knew what I had done? The store manager told me the President of McDonald's personally called to thank him . . . and he called him "Sir!"

So how does this translate into real-world Customer Service? I hope everyone who reads this manual can take away a special feeling about the commitment you share in the success of your company's Customer Service.

Try-Angles

Customer Service! The name implies the Customer is going to receive Service. The question is the type and level of Service expected versus the level provided.

According to Jim:
To overcome the roadblocks to success, you have to go from failure to failure without losing any of your determination. Try, try, again.

Here are three examples of Customer Service that occurred in Chicago within the same day:

Example 1:
The day started with a trip to find a computer cable for my new Apple PowerBook. I normally would have ordered online, but my sales rep from an Internet computer supplier was of no help. I called two stores in the area and neither could help me. The reason? I'm a MAC user in a PC world.

I went looking for some help. Actually, I went to pick up my stereo, which had been repaired, or so I thought. My first stop was Best Buy. I waited while three repair reps dealt with personal issues, talked with their friends, or flirted with each other. Several of us were kept waiting until Ian, the manager of the department, arrived. Suddenly, everyone was ready and willing to assist those of us waiting for Service.

Ian took care of me. He looked up the claim and asked why I had canceled the repair. I said Best Buy called to say the repair was completed and, because I had paid $30 in advance, there was no charge. After considerable research, Ian found the product claim and retrieved the unit. Prior to leaving, he offered to refund the $30 deposit because the repair was no charge. *WOW! Free repairs*, I thought.

When the unit was placed on the counter, I asked Ian if he would plug it in to make sure it worked (the reason for the repair was no power went to the unit). Nothing happened. No lights. And on the back of the unit was a notice that said the repair had been canceled. By whom? Certainly not by me. And certainly not by anyone in my office.

I was told I had to fill out a new repair ticket, return the $30 deposit, and then wait for another call with the estimated costs for repair. A total waste of my time. And, because the closest Best Buy is about 20 minutes from my home, making these needless trips was inconvenient at best.

The personnel were pleasant, but somewhat unconcerned. Comments such as, "It's out of our hands," "You know the guys in repair can't read," and "This happens all the time" certainly didn't give me a feeling of professionalism or concern. I received neither Customer Service nor repair Service. I felt I was just another interruption in their day.

Example 2:

On the way home, I saw a sign for a computer store: Micro Center—The Computer Department Store.

On entering the store, I was greeted by John, who was restocking shelves. John stopped his process and asked how he could help me. The way John asked indicated I was in the right place. "Is there something specific you need today?" *How clever,* I thought. Not the generic, "May I help you?" which is always answered by "No, just looking." This was a question that really required an answer, which opened a world of possibilities for both of us. "Yes!" I answered. "I need some assistance with my new Apple PowerBook."

"Certainly!" That response wasn't what I was programmed to expect. Not only was I surprised, but what followed was totally unexpected. John put down his inventory and walked me to the APPLE DEPARTMENT. Can you imagine? An APPLE DEPARTMENT!

My history with Apple goes back to the '80s. During the early years, I couldn't find anyone who even knew Apple was selling computers! My only resource had been online. Local stores, no matter how large, all treated Apple as the last dying breed of a bygone era. This was a time when Atari, Osborne, and Commodore were the innovative companies, and software developers like Ashton-Tate were larger than Microsoft. Not since the demise of vinyl records, 8-tracks, and $2 movies had a company like Apple lost so much consumer recognition and market share.

Yet, with the reintroduction of the exiled founder Steve Jobs, Apple once again commanded a small army of loyal enthusiasts who chose to remain mavericks in a PC world: new products, Lifesaver-like colors, and processing speeds that make most PCs look like tinker toys.

As we walked by towers of PC accessories, monitors, and ink jet printers, I noticed we were headed to a brightly lit room filled with Apple products. This was like entering another world. John quickly found someone to introduce me to and said his farewell with, "If there's anything you need or want that Eric can't find for you, please ask for me and I'll help you." With that, John extended his hand, shook mine, and departed like the proverbial genie who had just granted one of my three wishes.

Before I could say "Shazam!" Eric shook my hand, introduced himself, and asked, "How may I assist you today?" I quickly recovered from my shock and provided my own assault of questions. One by one, Eric answered them. Each reply addressed solutions, recommendations, and personal comments as to what to do, how to do it, and what to avoid. This was like the first time I was kissed by a woman without asking to be kissed! It was wonderful. It was pleasant. And I wanted more! I asked, Eric responded.

I was suddenly an adult in Disneyland. I had an E ticket to all the rides. Portable hard drives, flat screen monitors, auxiliary batteries, thumb drives, wireless keyboards, and more—and I had a gentle and knowledgeable guide. This felt like the time my father took me outside with my new bike and said, "When you're ready, we'll remove the training wheels. It's time for you to ride your bike like an adult." And so it happened.

I went in to buy a cable, expecting to pay $25–$50 and I found a substitute manufacturer made what I needed for only $8.95. With my savings, I spent over $800 in new tools and accessories for my laptop. But, more important, I found a resource, a solution to all my problems. I was in Customer Service Heaven. Nothing compared. John, my genie, was the savior of my computer problem.

As I left the department and went to the cashier, John reappeared. "Let me help you with all that," he said. John brought over a cart, loaded it, and asked if I had found everything I'd needed.

John took me to the checkout counter. A long line at three registers made it look like I'd be there a long time. Without a word, he took me to a closed register. "Wait here," John said, and then he called a young woman over to open the register. "We don't want you to have to wait any longer than it takes for her to check you out today. Thank you for your business." I immediately asked for John's card. "Sorry," he told me, "I just started here and I don't have one yet." Can you believe this?

Here it was—nirvana. A new hire who was well trained, Customer friendly, knowledgeable, and more. I couldn't contain myself. I gave John my card and told him I would appreciate it if he'd let me buy him lunch or something. I told him he'd been fabulous. And, as if a puff of smoke had whisked him away, John said, "Just doing my job, but thanks anyway."

I left the store with renewed vigor in the hope that everyone could learn from my experience. I planned, in my head, how to write this story and to add it to this manual. I was thrilled. That was then. This is now.

According to Jim:
Your clients aren't concerned with yesterday's accomplishments or what you did today. It's tomorrow that really matters to them.

Example 3:
My last stop took this feeling of euphoria away in the same flash that created it. I went to the US Post Office on Dearborn Street in Chicago. I have a mailbox there and needed to purchase some stamps. In addition, I wanted to exchange prepaid postcards to the same value in Forever Stamps before their cost went up. A simple task, or so I thought.

After waiting in line for 15 minutes, I presented myself to a clerk who recognized me. She and I exchanged salutations and I placed my unopened deck of postcards in front of her. I explained that my former assistant had made a mistake and purchased postcards instead of stamps for postcards. I wanted to exchange them for the same value of stamps.

"Sorry, no can do!"

"I don't understand," I answered. This is the post office and these are stamped postcards issued by the post office. What do you mean you can't exchange them?"

I was told 1) I needed a receipt, and 2) the receipt had to be from the Dearborn Street Post Office because the exchange policy was only for items sold at the same location, and 3) these were "old" postcards.

The Customer Service pendulum swung quickly from one side to the other. Only moments before, I'd had a magical Customer experience. Now, I was in government apathy hell. Not only was I shocked, I also couldn't understand. This wasn't some department store. And it wasn't some local business. This was the US Government Post Office, the federal agency that issues and sells postage stamps.

Mine was a simple request: take back unused postcards and give me the cash amount in stamps. Without asking, my nemesis beckoned for her supervisor, who told me returns weren't permitted. She also said the photo on the postcards was no longer the current photo, so it would difficult to sell those postcards to someone else. Further, in absence of a receipt from that particular post office, no exchange could be allowed.

Once again, I pleaded my case. 1) I didn't need postcards with stamps; I needed stamps for postcards. 2) What difference did it make where I purchased the postcards? The US Post Office sold them and I assumed the US Post Office was one big happy family, and 3) I wasn't asking for a refund, I was asking for an even exchange.

With one sweeping gesture, the supervisor said, "I don't have time to debate this with you. You aren't going to get a refund." After torpedoing me, she left to finish her submarine sandwich.

Today, I rank the US Post Office as one of the top three WORST CUSTOMER SERVICE companies in the US. It's too hard to determine which is worse on any given day: CitiMortgage, The US Post Office, or Comcast Business.

I just gave you three examples, three experiences. Three reasons how or why business isn't done. As I look back on how I was treated, the amount of tact, and the tone of each experience, I can only suggest that we all learn from the talent that trained the team members. Perhaps if Micro Center starts tackling postage stamps, they can teach our government how to stamp out the terrible temperament in our thankless postal system. Perhaps a new tradition could be tweaked that teaches our government employees and that tabulates treatment of its Customers. Later in this manual, I provide horror stories about my other two WORST CUSTOMER SERVICE companies: Comcast Business and CitiMortgage.

According to Jim:
All businesses exist to create, Service, and retain Customers, while making a profit as they deliver exceptional Service.

I had the pleasure of meeting and interacting with James Gilmore, co-author of *The Experience Economy*. In his book, Gilmore said, "Goods and Services are no longer enough." In his update edition, he said, "Perhaps not enough people read the line, let alone took it to heart." I can't say it any better.

Service excellence hasn't gotten better. It has become polarized. A few companies are great and they command great profits, better retention, and overall greater Customer Satisfaction. The others seem to exist because they either have monopolies in their chosen marketplace or they own the technology or they have no or little competition.

The good news is that product quality, overall, is higher. China, as an example, makes many disposable products. They don't Service them; they replace them. Outstanding Customer Service, from my standpoint, is unknown by most manufacturing in China, but that shouldn't translate into the US distributors taking the same approach. Currently, outstanding Customer Service is the only hope for unacceptable product quality because defective products aren't always designed to be Customer-friendly.

If rules and procedures are getting in the way of great Customer Service in your organization, maybe it's time for some shifts in thinking.

Tailor

17) Every Customer is a real person. Treat them as such.

What are their needs and how well are you addressing those needs? Customers want respect and honesty in all aspects of their dealings with your business. Treat your Customers as real, feeling, individual human beings and you'll discover hundreds of ways to form lasting Customer relationships.

Tweak

18) Every Customer has their own reason for complaining.

You must let the Customer tell their story. Don't interrupt. Don't respond until the Customer has told their version of the situation. At that point, my favorite response is, "What would you like me to do to solve this problem?" Each Customer has their own solution and there's no point in trying to second-guess it. What's so interesting is that many Customers have no idea how to answer that question.

Talent

19) Talent is the shortest route to providing great Customer Service.
- Define the problem
- Gather Information
- Create Alternatives
- Evaluate the Alternatives

Take Action

Talented people don't waste time. They utilize these five steps to reach a quick, agreeable resolution to the Customer's problem. No matter what is the resolution, it takes talent to reach it quickly.

20) Innovation is the ultimate problem solver.

Don't worry about what the proper procedure is if your company allows for creative problem solving. Improve the quality of the Customer Service relationship by injecting creativity in everything you do.

- Associate with creative people.
- Think of yourself as a creative person.
- Try to work for a company that maintains an environment that promotes creativity.
- Cultivate a sense of wonder by comparing what other companies do when faced with Customer Service issues.

21) Try to offer unique implantations that result in a better way to do something.

While you may be casual in your interactions with each other, you are focused and serious about the operations of your business. You believe in working hard and putting in the extra effort to get things done. Believe in operational excellence and realize there's always room for improvement in everything you do. This means your work is never done. To stay ahead of the competition (or would-be competition), you need to continuously innovate, as well as make incremental improvements to your operations, always striving to make yourself more efficient, always trying to learn how to do something better. Use mistakes as learning opportunities. Never lose your sense of urgency in making improvements. And never settle for "good enough," because good is the enemy of great.

According to Jim:

It's time to achieve Customer Insistence, remain viable and competitive, and create a more constant flow of solutions.

Action Summary

1. Set yourself apart from the competition. Give your Customers something they can't get elsewhere. Make your niche something of real value. Repeat Customers are your most profitable business asset.

2. Don't waste time on activities that can be automated. On the other hand, concentrate on the reason you're in business, which is your Customer. Firsthand experience isn't something you get secondhand. Make knowing your Customers a priority.

3. Eliminate the time you spend on nonproductive tasks. For instance, unsubscribe to newsletters you never read instead of deleting them each time. Handle paperwork one time, and then file it, instead of stacking it in a pile. All these little things add up to wasted time, which could be spent on your Customer.

4. Concentrate your efforts on marketing to the people who need your care. Start by auditing your marketing and sales data to find out how and why a sale is made. Eliminate or change your marketing strategies and Services that don't serve the needs of your Customers.

5. Respond to email quickly. Response time should be under 24 hours. By responding quickly, you send the message that your Customers are important and you're genuinely interested in meeting their needs. Our corporate policy is to reply the same day. In fact, we reply within four hours. Too often, companies don't respond to Customer inquires in less than several days, if at all.

6. Follow up on all sales orders. Your job is to make sure your Customers are thoroughly satisfied with their purchases. At that point, you can offer additional Services related to their purchases.

7. Give refunds promptly and unconditionally. No matter what your policy.

8. Make sure your Customers know what to expect. If you're going to refund everything but the shipping and handling, make sure your Customer understands that policy.

9. Ask your Customers to fill out a survey, so you can better understand their needs. Offer a valuable freebie or a discounted Service for participating. This strategy establishes a dialogue between you and your Customer, and it helps determine the direction of your business.

10. Publish a newsletter, write articles, give advice. Give your subscribers valuable tips and information they can't get anywhere else. Offer subscriber-only discounts and freebies.

11. Make doing business with your company easy. Your Customers' time is a valuable commodity. Customers appreciate finding what they want quickly and effortlessly.

Ten Ways to Treat Your Customers to the Ultimate in Customer Service!

1. Ensure a long-term, beneficial relationship by handling your clients respectfully, individually, and attentively.
2. Excellent Customer Service must be cultivated through ongoing proper guidance, and coordination of people and procedures.
3. Set up your Service to deliver answers and solutions when the Customer needs it. . . . NOW!
4. Realize that it takes everyone involved to consistently produce superior Customer Service.
5. Deal immediately with problems and negative issues while they're fresh and still somewhat small.
6. Show your Customers you appreciate their business by asking for their feedback, and then listen to them.
7. Deliver exceptional Customer Service and solutions. By treating the Customer the way you want to be treated, you enhance the value of every transaction.
8. Treat every Customer uniquely. One Size Does *Not* Fit All.
9. Aim high by setting the standards for professionalism and Service in your industry.
10. Learn from how others are treated. Learn from experience. Remain open-minded and always recognize that fitting your Customer's needs to a *T* is your ultimate goal.

Remember, D A T I N G Is Fun!

James Feldman

I Is for INNOVATION

22 Ways To Innovate Your Customer Service Solutions

> "Wealth in the new regime flows directly from innovation, not optimization; that is, wealth is not gained by perfecting the known, but by imperfectly seizing the unknown."
> —Kevin Kelly, *New Rules for the New Economy: 10 Radical Strategies for a Connected World*

Impress

1) If you aren't aggressively trying to innovate, you are managing your company toward extinction.

For most companies, innovation is an acquired taste, something to be learned and something that must be cultivated. The difference between a skill and an attitude is this: skills are taught and attitudes are caught.

Apathy is the main reason businesses don't work and complacency means your days are numbered. If your company scores low on creativity and innovation, you might not be around for the long term. And, of course, the same is true of personal relationships. While you were excited at the beginning of a new relationship, as time passed, familiarity began to create complacency. And complacency is often the reason couples break up and marriages end in divorce.

Innumerable

2) Competitive advantage can be described as being Number One.

No one remembers Number two. Who won the silver or bronze metal? Who came in second in the World Series, the Super Bowl, etc.?

Another example: take the Internet and search engines. Search engines are used to find products or Services that have a website on the Internet. Every company wants to be Number One on search engines like Yahoo! or Excite. This means the search engine places your company at the top of the search list. Yet, being Number One doesn't assure success. In fact, it could mean you're spending so much time trying to be Number One that you forget your core basics are running your business and satisfying your Customers.

According to Jim:
Think about "Clear and Present" opportunities, and then become a solution provider.

Ideology

3) Being Number One with your Customers means they will tell others.

Being Number One is a great goal if it has some business merit. Your Customers will brag about how they found you. They'll tell others about how well you treat them. And, if you still doubt the power of the Internet, you'll soon find out how quickly your Customers will tell the world. Will your company receive positive or negative feedback? Consider what your Customers could say if they feel you've done something wrong or if you don't deliver exceptional Customer Service. They'll tell everyone who will listen. They'll log on to chat sites, tell everyone on their email list, and stop doing business with you, while advising others to do the same. Your goal is to forget about search engines.

Instead, find Customers and give them the best possible Customer Service. The more satisfied your Customers are, the more business you'll have in the future.

> "Of the 100 largest United States companies at the beginning of the twentieth century, only 16 are identifiable today. Considering more recent history, of the companies in the Fortune 500 in 1970, one-third had ceased to exist by the early 1980s. And during the 1980s, a total of 230 companies—46 percent—disappeared from the Fortune 500. Obviously, neither size nor reputation guarantees continued success or survival."
>
> —*Strategy & Business Journal*

Can you guess how many of the corporations we knew in 2000 are still in business?

Can you say:
- Toys"R"Us
- Sears
- Blockbuster
- EF Hutton
- TWA
- General Foods
- Compaq
- PaineWebber
- Pan Am
- Arthur Andersen
- Standard Oil

Here's more information from that same article.

IBM survived by listening to clients

If you look more closely at why IBM survived its near-death experience of 1993, it had little to do with funding big, expensive, long-term projects. At the time, IBM was losing more money than any company had ever lost in US history—US $8.10 billion loss for the 1992 financial year. On July 26, 2018, Facebook lost $119.4 billion. Shift Happens!®

This was because IBM's core mainframe business had been disrupted by the advent of the personal computer and the client server. IBM couldn't compete with smaller, nimbler, less-diversified competitors.

Then, IBM's CEO John F. Akers decided that the logical and rational solution was to split IBM into autonomous business units (such as processors, storage, software, Services, and printers), which could compete more effectively with competitors that were more focused and agile, and had lower cost structures. If IBM had continued to follow the Akers path, IBM wouldn't be celebrating its 100th birthday this year.

What happened was quite different. After Akers was fired as CEO, IBM hired Louis V. ("Lou") Gerstner, Jr. as the new CEO. It was the first time since 1914 that IBM recruited a leader from outside its ranks. Even more striking was the fact that Gerstner had no background in computing.

Not knowing much about computing per se, Gerstner had the good sense to start listening to clients. Gerstner discovered the biggest problem all the big companies were facing in 1993 was in integrating all the separate computing technologies emerging at the time.

So, while continuing to cut costs, Gerstner reversed the move to spin off IBM business units into separate companies. Having understood IBM's Customers, Gerstner recognized that one of IBM's greatest strengths was its capability to provide integrated solutions for Customers—a firm that could represent more than piece parts or components—something he wouldn't have learned by listening to the proponents of different technologies within IBM. Splitting the company would have destroyed IBM's unique competitive advantage.

The key to long-term survival

IBM's experience is pivotal, as explained in Professor Ranjay Gulati's guide to long-term corporate survival, *Reorganize for Resilience*.

The thrust of Gulati's marvelous book is this: in today's white-water world of rapid change and massively enhanced Customer power, the only road to resilience is—like Gerstner at IBM—adopting an outside-in perspective by solving Clients' most pressing problems or finding unexpected ways to delight them.

Delighting clients isn't enough

Moreover, merely focusing on delighting clients won't be enough. That's because the hierarchical bureaucracy of the traditional Fortune

500 Company will undermine and ultimately kill single-fix initiatives to delight Customers.

According to Jim:
You have to use your head and think for yourself. If your product is faulty your price/value relationship is flawed or the product quality is short-lived. Delighting your Customers can't fix everything.

Idle

4) Innovate your Customer Service.

Think of your significant other and imagine an anniversary in which one of you forgot the present, the card, the flowers, or any acknowledgment of the relationship. Think how you would feel if you were the one who was forgotten. Do you think that feeling is any different if you're a Customer?

Did anyone thank you for your business? Did anyone ask you if you were happy with the product or Service? Innovative? Yes, based on the fact that so few companies do it at all.

Important

5) Make your Customer feel important and your Customer will do the same for you.

Everyone likes to be thought of as important. Even more important, show your Customers how your product or Service can benefit them.

Show your Customer how they will look better, feel better, do their job better, or enjoy life better. Show them how you can save them time.

Make the experience one in which Customers realize their lives would be better with your product.

> "The world's greatest Customer-oriented strategy: 'Don't tell me how good you make it, tell me how good it makes me when I use it.'"
>
> —Leo Burnett, advertising guru

Ignite

6) Every company that plans to compete in the twenty-first century needs to develop new ideas and next-generation approaches.

Customers are no longer stuck with one resource or supplier. The Internet has opened the entire world to Customers who can surf and find what they want, for the price they want, with the Service level they expect. So, leaders and managers must create a new accountability:

- The Customer is king and now knows it.
- New products aren't an option.
- New ways of doing business are being created each day.
- The Customer votes with their dollars.
- The playing field has changed. You must change with it.
- The company that's successful today must meet competition head-on and be better than its competitor or lose the battle.

> "In three years, every product my company makes will be obsolete. The only question is whether we'll make them obsolete or somebody else will."
>
> —Bill Gates, *Business @ the Speed of Thought: Succeeding in the Digital Economy*

Innovate

7) Management must foster a climate open to innovation.

The management team must set the stage for innovation and creative thinking. Creativity is the ability of the human mind to come up with ideas and solutions to pressing problems. It's the process of producing something that a) has value, and b) didn't exist before.

> "Innovating has become the most urgent concern of corporations everywhere."
> —Kenneth Larson, author, *Fortune* magazine

Remember, failure and innovation are related. A safety zone needs to be created for failure, experimentation, and more failure. Success only comes when you learn from failure.

Insecure

8) You must know your business better than your competitor.

On a typical day, which of the following takes up most of your time?

- Dealing with difficult people
- Coming up with productive ideas
- Accomplishing little in meetings
- Using skills to achieve corporate objectives

> **As you learn to solve problems, ask yourself...**
>
> What issues or questions can you create to rattle the cages of the people you work with (including yourself)?
>
> Can you honestly say that, without serious attention to some of these issues, your organization can continue to grow, combat competition, and maintain profitability?
>
> If your idea were a football team, what would be your strongest and weakest positions?
>
> Who would be able to solve your most stubborn work problem: a master psychologist, a venture capitalist, or an enforcer for the mob?

Identify

9) Each day, you are removed from the decision maker and put in front of a gatekeeper.

Today's management just isn't what it used to be. And, tomorrow, the person you talk to won't be the decision maker. You must motivate the person you're speaking to *now*. Then you can get to the next person—who will manage even less and care even less about you, but who will care more about what you can do for their career. The key to all these processes is to identify the decision maker and chart a path to reach that person. Until you get to the decision maker, most of your efforts will be spent dealing with someone who can't be your Customer.

We work best these days when we function as thinkers—independent problem solvers—rather than waiting for higher levels of management to do our thinking for us. So, you need to stay in alignment with the objectives of organizations. You must put forth more effort to get the sale. Whether you lose the sale because of indifference or because you were too aggressive doesn't matter. In both cases, you lost the sale. You need to build trust with your Customer. You need to be your Customer's best solution to the current business problem. You aren't giving away the store. You aren't negotiating a lower price without getting something in return. Make sure you're selling what you believe is the best solution. And, if you aren't, move away and focus on something else. For you to sell, you need to be highly trustworthy. People buy from people they trust and like.

According to Jim:
We can't survive the twenty-first century with the innovations from the twentieth century. Shift Happens!® and we need to embrace it.

Inoculate

10) No matter what you're selling, you are the only commodity your Customer will know.

Pretend you need the money or your kids won't eat. Pretend if you don't get the sale, you'll be out on the street. Pretend you have the cure for cancer and you must get your patient to accept a nontraditional approach you are certain will work.

You are personally accountable to your Customer.

You're the catalyst who is bringing both together. You need to invest more time in data exchange and do more to keep the channels of communication open. Then your Customer will buy from you.

"Research shows that creativity can be taught and companies are listening."
—Business Week

Impress

11) Help Create Value.

Organizations exist to create value for stakeholders.

Who is the stakeholder in the organization? Is that person the decision-maker? Find that person. You are trying to offer value that will beat the competition. You do this by providing answers or solutions to problems that slowed the process of building the organization or increasing profitability in either their personal or corporate return on investment. Value creation must be part of your culture.

You must weave it into your daily work habits and communication. This needs to influence your work consciousness at every level . . . and you need to foster this need on your clients.

Ask questions instead of selling. Understand your Customer's needs first, and then find a solution. Listen, don't talk. This could be the greatest innovation you have in your organization—the ability to listen.

Clarify which activities—not costs—drive value in the minds of your Customers. No one will complain about your prices if you can show your Customers you're a worthwhile investment with a large return on their interest.

According to Jim:
Wealth isn't gained by perfecting the known, but by seizing the unknown and taking charge of your own destiny.

Interrogate

12) Value is created by how well the people on the front line do their jobs.

To understand this, you must find out how you can have a positive influence on the value drivers. Be conscious of how your product or Service might cut costs, increase productivity, or generate more cash. What can you do to boost productivity? Build sales? Delight your client's Customers? Think like the owner. Think like you own the business. Think about the person you're talking to and ask yourself why they're listening.

The truth is this: value gets determined deep inside organizations by people just like you. These people have a life. They might have a family. Value creation occurs at all levels. Decisions don't!

At the same time, people ask, "What's in it for me?" "Why should I care?" Your job is to make your Customer's (your employee, in this case) job more secure. You have to show your Customer you won't let them down. Your success depends on their success. You are a partner, not a vendor. The creation of value, and your contribution to it, is the very thing that delivers the paycheck.

Raising your client's prosperity is the surest way to raise your own.

> **"When a man pursues a woman, he is interacting in a manner that says he is interested in finding out if he is the one for her. '... I could fulfill your needs. I could do things to make you really happy....'"**
>
> —John Gray, *Mars and Venus on a Date: A Guide for Navigating the 5 Stages of Dating to Create a Loving and Lasting Relationship*

Intensify

13) The pursuit of a partnership in D-A-T-I-N-G is really no different than the same pursuit for Customers or the need to find a supplier of goods or Services to fulfill a specific need. The nature of both is offering a promise and delivering on that promise. The recipient is then asked to respond in some manner that either encourages the continuation of the relationship—more dates or more business—or the discontinuation of it.

Nearly every adult has been in a relationship at least once in their life and Customer relationships take place every day. All business transactions and all dates are based on someone delivering a promise to fulfill a specific desire or need. So, when you compare innovation in either situation, you can readily see that lack of follow-through or poor attitudes can impact the relationship more than the event or product itself. "I am neither for nor against apathy," quipped one of the famous comedians who used to perform in the Catskills.

Today, that same attitude can be found in both large companies and small ones. Companies exist that spend millions of dollars promoting their Services only to make the Customer wait on hold or have to redial numerous times to lodge complaints. This is the same with dating. Spending money doesn't assure you success. And times have changed. With role reversal in play today—where a woman now feels comfortable asking a man out on a date—has a woman's sensitivity become more the standard in dating? Has a woman's ability to have a softer side convinced a man that dating isn't a hedonistic ritual followed by courtship, marriage, family, and, often, divorce? Does any information show you, when the roles are reversed, a woman makes better decisions when trying to pursue the opposite sex? I think not. Throughout history we have all made mistakes. Whether the man is initiating the date or the woman has accepted that role, mistakes are mistakes.

Ingenious

14) The best you can hope for is to learn from your mistakes.

Explore your attitude toward mistakes by contemplating what you learned or how you reacted. Ask yourself:

1. What did I learn about making mistakes?
2. What role does fear play in making mistakes at my company?
3. What role does fear play in making mistakes in my personal life?
4. What would I do differently if I had no fear or felt no repercussion would occur from my making a mistake?

Incredible

Consider the fate of China and recognize each of us has to learn from our mistakes and adversity. We must use the information to innovate and stimulate our quest for improvement at all levels.

James Feldman

"At the outset of the fifteenth century, China with its curiosity, its instinct for exploration, and its drive to build had created all the technologies necessary to launch the Industrial Revolution, something that would not actually occur for another 400 years. It had the blast furnace and piston bellows for making steel (the amount of pig iron that China produced annually in the late eleventh century would not be matched anywhere in the world for 700 years); gunpowder and the cannon for military conquest; the compass and the rudder for exploration; paper and movable type for printing; the iron plough, the horse collar, rotary threshing machines, and mechanical seeders to generate agriculture surpluses; the ability to drill for natural gas; and, in mathematics, the decimal system, negative numbers, and the concept of zero, which put the Chinese far ahead of the Europeans. Large Chinese armadas carrying as many as 28,000 men were exploring Africa's east coast about the same time that Portugal and Spain were sending much smaller expeditions down the west coast of Africa. Seven major Chinese expeditions explored the Indian Ocean with ships four times as large as those of Columbus.

But the geographic conquests and the Industrial Revolution that were possible did not happen. The Chinese rejected and ultimately forgot the technologies that could have given them world dominance. New technologies were perceived as threats rather than opportunities. Innovation was forbidden. Imperial edicts prohibited the building of new ocean-going ships and sailing away from the Chinese coastline. By the end of the fifteenth century, the demand for order had overridden intrinsic human curiosity, the desire to explore, and the drive to build."

—Lester Thurow, MIT economist, *Atlantic Monthly*, June 1999

Ignite

15) Innovation is a creative solution used by people other than the person who created it.

The world we live in today first existed in the ideas within the minds of men—bridges, skyscrapers, automobiles, religions, philosophies, governments, symphonies, paintings, poems—everything. But these ideas didn't remain mental images. They were put into action. Risks were taken to turn thoughts into reality.

Most solutions might be better understood if you think in terms of inventing/innovating instead of creating. A certain risk is involved for both parties, just like asking someone out on a date. Each person must take some reasonable risk-taking. Each person is trying to explore, to think, to act like a partner, while really being a pioneer. The quickest way to stop a person from being a risk-taker is to punish that person's efforts or to remind them of a failure. If everyone determines that stepping out, pushing the envelope, or trying something new is too risky, no one can survive. Creativity is normally regarded as something that breaks conventions and not as something that operates within the framework of existing conventions. We must foster a climate that's open to innovation.

And with these innovative attempts comes failure. Remember, failure and innovation are related. A safety zone needs to be created for failure. Success only comes when you learn from failure.

Indisputable

16) You must create affirmations that help guide you down the path on the way to enlightenment.

Dating is like a form of innovation. Each time you go out, you learn what you like or dislike. From one relationship to the next, you're taken on a journey of learning, comparison, and, yes, frustration. You're often surprised to find the person who's physically less-than-perfect is a warmer, more sensitive, and more caring person than someone you've been fantasizing about for years. You learn the best dancer isn't a swimsuit model or a body-building hunk but, instead, wears glasses or a bow tie. If you're too critical or try to turn each "date" into your preconceived description, then you'll never experience all the world has to offer. The quest for knowledge opens the door to freedom. It helps all of us understand each other and provides what's best for each of us, personally or in business.

> "The problem is never how to get new innovative thoughts into your mind, but how to get old ones out of it."
> —Dee Ward Hock, creator of Visa

Your company must support innovation and creativity. To offer exceptional Customer Service, you can't be bound by the "we always did it this way" syndrome. You must constantly redesign your company's "rules" to be flexible and show that you, as a company, value worthy ideas, no matter what the source.

You must give people, whether you're dating them or working with them, positive reinforcement. You must show people that bringing their imagination on the journey is welcome. Information wealth flows directly from innovation, not optimization. Wealth, of any kind, isn't gained by perfecting the known, but by seizing the unknown. We must all become serial producers of ideas, concepts, and innovations. We need to try them out to see if they work. If we don't, we'll lose out to our competitors.

Illustrate

17) The more offbeat, the more diverse, eccentric, and unusual, the more you learn.

As you started dating—no matter how young—you usually included people with diverse perspectives because experience thrives on multiple points-of-view. Relationships often didn't work, but you learned from them. You learned what you liked and disliked. And, without that experience, how could you learn what was right for you? Or what worked? You needed mavericks. You needed to know renegades.

John Francis ("Jack") Welch, Jr., renowned former Chairman and CEO at General Electric, regarded by many as one of the greatest business leaders of the era, distilled his years of experience and wisdom into six basic tenets. They were the underpinnings of the changes he brought about at G.E. These became know as "Jack Welch's Six Rules." They are:

1. Face reality as it is, not as it was, or as you wish it were.
2. Be candid with everyone.
3. Don't manage, lead.
4. Change before you have to.
5. If you don't have a competitive advantage, don't compete.
6. Control your own destiny, or someone else will."

—Neil H. Snyder and Angel P. Clontz, *The Will to Lead: Managing with Courage & Conviction in the Age of Uncertainty*

Years ago, anyone with a tattoo was considered a rebel. Now tattoos are thought of as fashion statements. Body piercing—once relegated to gang members, hoodlums, and less-desirable personalities—has given way to what some consider sexy and alluring. Placement of tattoos has become more of a representation of tactile gratification. While many of us question the need or use of tattoos, it's fair to say they're increasing, rather than decreasing, in acceptance.

Insentient

18) We need to demand more from ourselves than from our Customers.

We all need to stretch ourselves. We all need to innovate in everything we do. We need to examine dramatic and new approaches, and to treat every complaint as a learning opportunity. Instead of reacting to a situation, use it to build an arsenal of information that makes you better at what you do for your Customer.

James Feldman

"In this volatile business of ours, we can ill-afford to rest on our laurels, even to pause in retrospect. Times and conditions change so rapidly that we must keep our aim constantly on the future."

—Walt Disney (1901–1966)

Influence

19) Learn constructively.

I often hear people complain about their organization's constraints, limitations, and regimens. Instead of complaining, though, think about using those constraints, limitations, and regimens to accept, analyze, and refine whenever possible. Be innovative.

On my eighteenth birthday, I sent my mother a dozen roses. The card read, "Congratulations! Heard you had a boy!" My mother was so thrilled, she told everyone—my father, sisters, neighbors. Anyone who would listen. The next day, I got a call from the mother of a girl I wanted to date. She told me her daughter had broken up with her boyfriend and I should come over for dinner. She had heard about the roses from my mother and she hoped her daughter would find the same kind of thoughtfulness. That meeting lead to dating her daughter for quite some time. In fact, we dated until she moved to another part of the country.

I realized then that even your mother's influence is important to your social life.

I continued to send flowers to my mother every birthday. And, since that time, she got me a summer job, a date with the homecoming queen, an internship, and an introduction to a US Ambassador. Every time my birthday approached, my mother started to tell everyone—her hairdresser, her delivery person, the person who washed the car, and others. Often they would ask to meet this "innovative" young man. I became known as "The Bright Idea Guy" and that still sticks today.

Institute

20) Remove "standard operating procedures" and inspire clever solutions to any problem.

> "In such a chaotic and complex environment, where changes and crises occur so rapidly, how can any organization hope to create a specific set of rules governing employee behavior? Most innovative organizations are replacing rules with roles, creating a strong sense of purpose and a clear understanding of goals and mission, and leaving employees to their own devices, absent rigidity."
>
> —Richard W. Oliver, *The Shape of Things to Come: 7 Imperatives for Winning in the New World of Business*

I'm frequently reminded that my dates, and the dates of others, didn't always work out. I always tried to remain a gentleman, though, even during and after a break up. This often led my ex to introduce me to someone else. There's no reason to burn bridges. Today, this would mean being nice to everyone you meet. You never know when a merger will take place and you could find yourself working for your ex.

Remember your first date? Remember your start-up operation? Use novel approaches, dramatic results, and reach for the highest goal possible.

21st Century Management must WOW them, not *why* them.

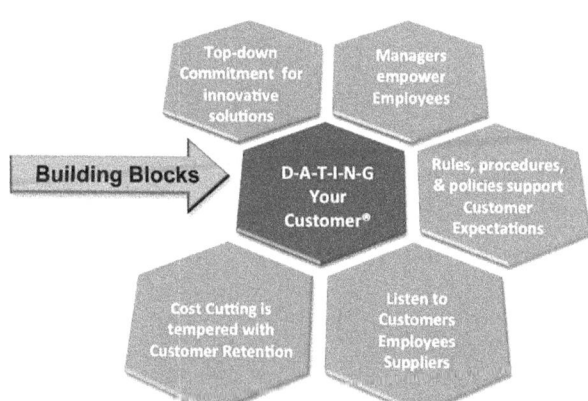

Imitate

21) Innovation is how you make money from creativity.

Look for a fresh perspective that, almost by itself, makes the solution obvious. You are the expert of your business. Problems do have solutions, but the solutions aren't always in plain site. Remember, creativity is the skill to originate the new and make it valuable. Innovation is the process of creating something new that has significant value. But before innovation, you must have creativity.

For more information on how to be more innovative, refer to my 3Thinking: Using Try Angles For Innovative Problem Solving at www.shifthappens.com.

> "Peter Parker tells a story about a cab driver that contains a valuable lesson for anyone in business. Parker once flew into Dallas for a business meeting with a client. When he stepped out of the terminal, a spotless cab pulled up immediately. The driver leapt out of the cab, rushed to open the passenger door for Parker, and made sure he was comfortably seated before closing the door. As the cabby got into the driver's seat, he told Parker that the neatly folded copy of the *Wall Street Journal* in the back seat was for him; then he showed Parker several cassette tapes, and asked what kind of music he would like to listen to. Finally, Parker could no longer resist. He said to the cabby, 'Obviously, you take great pride in your work. You must have a story to tell.'
>
> Indeed he did. The cabby told Parker that, for years, he toiled in corporate America. Eventually, he got tired of thinking that his best would not be good enough. So he decided to find a niche in life where he could be proud of being the best he could be every single day. He made a list of everything he enjoyed: he loved driving cars, being of care to people, and feeling like he had done a full day's worth of work at the end of the day. Guess what? He decided to become a cab driver—the very best car driver he could be. He bases his work on one thing: to be good in the cab-

driving business, he simply has to meet the expectations of his passengers. But to be the best, he would have to exceed Customer's expectations. So that is what he does with everyone who gets in his cab."

—Jack Canfield and Jacqueline Miller, adapted from, *Heart at Work: Stories and Strategies for Building Self-Esteem and Reawakening the Soul at Work*

Innovation is disruptive in most organizations because they do business-as-usual (BAU). While it's true, in part, innovation is more likely to succeed if small steps are taken. It's like losing weight. You can't wake up one day and say... "Poof.... 50 pounds are gone." Placing big bets is only good if you're winning at the local casino. Otherwise, the real question is how much disruptive innovation do you really need to advance your business goals while not being blocked by BAU?

Incremental changes, while possibly disruptive, improve the chances of success. Like losing weight, you put it on slowly, and then take it off slowly. Stop being transactional and become transformational. Test the waters. You'll quickly learn how much disruption is too much disruption.

Irreplaceable

"In order to be irreplaceable, one must always be different."
—Coco Chanel

Regardless of the industry, with few exceptions, the creation of a Customer is a lost art. The by-product of sameness and mediocrity is price sensitivity. For that reason, we default to expecting nothing, so we go for the best price. And the future under that philosophy is that companies like Amazon, Zappos, Apple, and Hyundai will grow, and mergers, bankruptcy, takeovers, and asset sell-offs will prosper. Similarly, give me one company that adopts the common sense techniques and knowledge in this manual, follows the six steps to D-A-T-I-N-G, and has a sufficient vision to manage for the long-term, and I'll show you a Customer-centric company.

> "No matter how they define the word, quality theorists hold one dictum paramount: give the Customer what they want. And the theorists recommend the following specific steps for achieving and maintaining Customer Satisfaction:
>
> 1. Give priority attention to Customers and their needs. Use Customer feedback to refine product designs, marketing strategies, and manufacturing processes.
>
> 2. Encourage managers to empower subordinates. A quality manager learns to trust subordinates and provides them with opportunities to handle responsibilities. The manager at the Baldrige-winning Milliken Company tells any employee who detects a quality or safety problem to halt the production process.
>
> 3. Emphasize improvement rather than maintenance. Small, daily, quality improvements yield better results than a leave well-enough alone attitude.
>
> 4. Make an enduring commitment to quality. Everyone in the organization must commit to quality. Progress should be measured against quality goals and the measurement tools themselves should be reexamined frequently."
>
> —Warren H. Schmidt, professor emeritus of business, University of Southern California, and Jerome P. Finnigan, *The Race Without a Finish Line: America's Quest for Total Quality.*

Every week, I write about innovation, Customer Service, leadership, and disruption on my website, www.shifthappens.com. My site has two sections, "According to Jim" and, within that tab, "LESSONS." I promise it will be worth your time. And, if you like me on Facebook and Tweet about me, I'll send you a nice gift as a thank you. So why not? Let's be disruptive together.

Action Summary

1. Stay in contact with your Customer regularly.
2. Show your Customer you're the consummate professional with extensive product knowledge.
3. Find a way to make your Customer start thinking about your Services.
4. Sell your Customer on ideas (rather than just products) by sharing proven case histories with them.
5. Make your Customer's research an enjoyable experience.
6. Make each one of your Customers know they are the most important Customer you have.
7. Innovate. Don't replicate.
8. Become transformational, not transactional, in everything you do.
9. Create smaller disruptions to test the ability to make shifts without resistance.
10. Innovation is the product of discomfort and the way we make money from creativity. Remember: it's not creative unless it sells. It must completely solve the problem without many resources or negative effects. Ideally, it becomes replicable, so others can use the effective solution.

Circles of Clarity

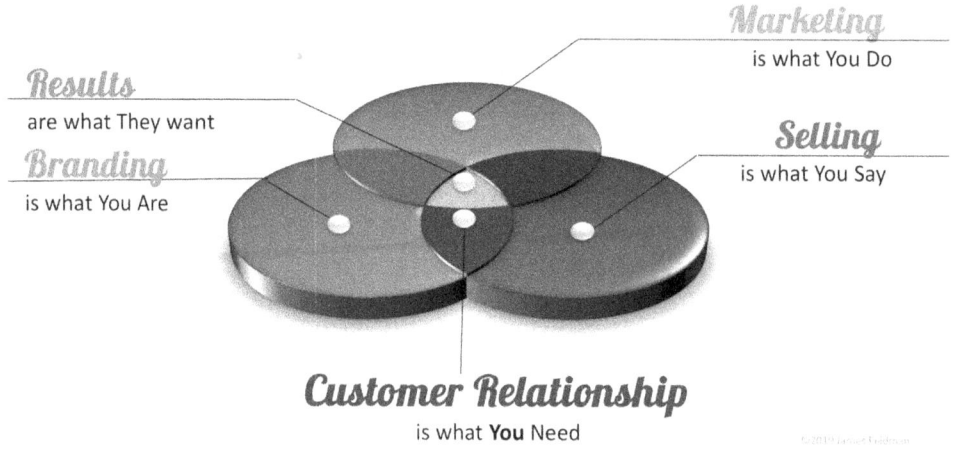

James Feldman

20 Concepts for Innovative Customer Service

1. If you aren't aggressively trying to innovate, you're managing your company toward extinction.
2. Competitive advantage can be described as being Number One.
3. Being Number One with your Customers means they'll tell others.
4. Innovate your Customer Service.
5. Make your Customer feel important and your Customer will do the same.
6. Every company that plans to compete in the twenty-first century needs to develop new ideas and next-generation approaches.
7. Management must foster a climate open to innovation.
8. You must know your business better than your competitor.
9. Each day, you're removed from the decision maker and in front of a "gatekeeper."
10. No matter what you're selling, *you* are what your Customer knows.
11. Help create value.
12. Value is created by how well the people on the front lines do their jobs.
13. The pursuit of a partnership in D•A•T•I•N•G is really no different than the same pursuit for Customers.
14. The best you can hope for is to learn from your mistakes.
15. Innovation is a creative solution used by people other than the person who created it.
16. You must create affirmations that help guide you down the path on the way to enlightenment.
17. The more off-beat, the more diverse, eccentric, and unusual, the more you learn.
18. You need to demand more from yourself than from your Customers.
19. Learn constructively.
20. Remove BAU and standard operating procedures. Inspire clever solutions to any problem.

N Is for Nurture

Nurture Your Internal Customers with 20 Ways to Create Great External Customer Service

The other chapters in this manual focus on external Customers, without whom you couldn't survive. Many of the principles of Customer Service discussed here also apply to internal Service issues. This chapter focuses on internal Customers—your employees—without whom you can't survive as an organization. Great Customer Service must be a total commitment from your company.

Every employee is also a Customer. Every Customer is someone who wants something in return for their action or payment to you. Once you've reached this point in the manual, you should understand that all relationships—business, family, social, and political—share a similar component: people. You can never predict the reaction of people. You can plan, hope, and communicate, but you can never forecast accurately.

You might notice only a few references appear to the dating comparison in this chapter. While I personally feel a great dating relationship is similar to working with and training your staff, too many negative implications currently exist, which could cause someone to take the comparison incorrectly. Enough said. If you're going to D•A•T•E your employee in the context of this manual, please be aware that the current climate isn't conducive to any language or actions that could be taken as sexual harassment.

Negligence

I was on board a Carnival cruise to the Caribbean. Within an hour after departure, we ran into a rainstorm. There was nothing to do but go back to my cabin. I turned on the TV, only to find it didn't work. The radio didn't work either. I called the cabin steward and was directed to the engineer, who told me that because of the storm, he couldn't come to my cabin for an hour or two. After I put down the phone, I decided to read. The purser called then. He apologized for the delay and the nonavailability of the engineer, and he offered to move me to another cabin. I explained I was fine, but that I appreciated the call. Ten minutes later, the cabin steward was at my door asking if the TV had been fixed. When I explained the situation, the steward offered to move me to another cabin, if only to be able to watch TV.

Almost as quickly as the rain started, it stopped. I went to dinner. On my return, I found a handwritten note from the television technician. He explained that the fuse in my cabin had been replaced and everything was now working. He left his beeper number in case I needed him again. While reading his note, a letter from the purser was slipped under my door. It read: "Mr. Feldman, I have been unable to reach you this evening by phone. My Service technician informs me that he has repaired your television and radio. If, for any reason, they aren't working, please call me at my direct extension." I was amazed.

Noteworthy

My problem had been a small one—certainly not one that required phone calls and handwritten notes. And, while I fully appreciated all the attention to my problem, on a larger scale, the crew's response spoke volumes for the training Carnival Cruise Lines provides to its thousands of employees.

I wrote a note to Robert Dickinson, then President of Carnival Cruise Lines. As I was sealing the envelope, I heard a knock at the door. The cabin steward held a bottle of champagne, a fruit-and-cheese platter, and a note from the captain of the ship. The captain apologized for the inconvenience and hoped my cruise would be "more than I expected" for its duration. It was. I told dozens of people about my experience. Carnival became my most-often used and recommended cruise line. And, of course, I booked another cruise on Carnival.

Necessary

None of this could have happened without the training, coworker involvement, and overall organizational goal of Customer Satisfaction. No one blamed the other person. Everyone acted like a team member. Everyone understood the role of others. This truly was a fantastic example of how to empower employees with internal Customer Service training that resulted in superior external Customer Service.

Notice

1) Internal Customers are your coworkers.

A company that understands how to expand the knowledge, commitment, and satisfaction of internal Customers is going to create happy external Customers.

Employees are often each other's Customers at different times. For example, mangers have to report payroll numbers properly—and on time—for the payroll department to do its job. In turn, the payroll department issues accurate checks, on time, for managers as well as other employees.

You are the Customer of people who work for you because you're dependent on them to do your job. And they're also your Customers because they depend on you for information, training, and support.

Nevertheless

2) Coworkers must interact before they can act on the behalf of a Customer.

If the interaction isn't positive, it's much harder for the external Customer to find a positive Customer Service experience. A happy employee can make the Customer happy. On the other hand, though . . .

Dissatisfied employees:

- Cost the company money.
- Give poor Customer Service.
- Recruit others to the "dark side."
- Bad-mouth your company to your Customers.

Having happy, satisfied employees translates to great Customer Service for the following reasons.

Happy employees:
- Like their jobs and project that attitude to Customers.
- Want the company to succeed and realize that taking care of Customers is the best way to insure they're role models for others.
- Find that when they're treated with respect, they want to treat Customers the same way.

According to the Gallup Organization's 2015–2017 State of the American Workplace Report:

- Only 33 percent of the American workers were engaged, involved in, enthusiastic about, and committed to their workplace.
- 16 percent of American workers are actively disengaged.
- Gallup estimates that actively disengaged employees cost the US $483 billion to $605 billion in lost productivity each year.
- Gallup research shows that companies with 11 engaged employees for every actively disengaged employee in 2014–2015 experienced a 115 percent higher earnings per share on average, compared with 2011–2012.
- Companies in the top quartile of employee engagement boast: 21% higher profitability, 17% higher productivity, 41% lower absenteeism, 59% lower turnover, and 10% higher customer metrics.

Nourish

3) A good internal Customer Service program can be achieved by education.

If you're encouraging your employees, you're developing their skills and self-esteem. This, in turn, increases the value of your employees to your organization, thereby increasing their value to your Customers.

Neighborly

4) Employees must work together to form a cohesive unit that can Service the Customers of a business.

Workplace conditions, education, and empowerment all contribute to satisfied internal Customers. A simple "thank you" between employees or supervisors can go a long way, but internal politics can kill external Service.

Necessity

5) "Yes" must" replace "No." "Can do" must replace "It's not my job."

Your company might be able to find good Service without an internal focus, but you'll never get your employees to go the extra mile unless they want to do so. Once your employees make the decision to go that extra mile, they'll continue to extend themselves by doing the best job possible.

Needs

In an attitude survey by Watson Wyatt Worldwide, well over 80 percent of the 9,144 polled respondents said they know their employers' goals and their duties. But 38 percent said they needed information or regular feedback. And only 55 percent had the power to make decisions to satisfy Customers.

Based on these responses, where do you think you should focus your efforts on keeping your Customers happy?

What Do Employees Want from Their Jobs?

An old sales rule states: when Customers tell you what they want, give it to them. Translate this rule to your organization. If we know what an internal Customer wants, we'll provide it. In either case, is it any different than a successful date? Within reason, satisfy the human need or want, and you have a friend for life. Recognize them and they'll be grateful.

Nice

6) A people-approach to business results in profits.

Many studies have shown that money isn't the biggest motivator for employees. But most bosses still find this hard to understand.

Look at the following box to see what employees want in their jobs—and what supervisors think employees want. Note the big discrepancy between employees' top three wants and supervisors' ratings of their importance.

What Employees Want In Their Jobs
as perceived by employees and supervisors

	Employees	Supervisors
Interesting Work	1	5
Appreciation	2	8
Feeling "in" on Things	3	10
Job Security	4	2
Good Pay	5	1
Promotions	6	3
Good Working Conditions	7	4
Personal Growth	8	7
Help w/ Personal Problems	9	9
Tactful Discipline	10	6

—George Mason University Survey
1 is highest importance, 10 is lowest importance.

Never-ending

7) **The objectives of great internal Customer Services are to do the following:**

- ♥ Retain existing employees and encourage them to come back to work each day. (Happier employees also save you money and perpetuate a positive culture by recruiting new applicants with similar attitudes and expectations.)
- ♥ Increase each employee's awareness of their need to exceed coworker expectations.
- ♥ Increase the commitment of each person to be responsible for coworker Satisfaction, as well as to revise policies and procedures whenever necessary to increase overall Satisfaction.
- ♥ Empower each employee with information and decision-making authority.
- ♥ Make the workplace a positive place.

The head of Starbucks feels part of his secret to success is to cultivate Customer contentment by exalting his employees. Schultz says, "Our people come first, then the Customers, and then the shareholder."

—Howard D. Schultz, Chairman and CEO of Starbucks

Nugget

8) This could sound like the wrong order, but you can't exceed the expectations of your Customers unless you first exceed your expectations for your employees.

We often forget our employees are also our Customers. We are selling them on the premise that we are a good company with a valuable product, offered at a fair price. We treat our Customers fairly—now we need to apply that same principle to our employees.

The best employees can be described as . . .

- Trustworthy
- Relationship-oriented
- Solution-minded
- Advocates for Customers
- Action-oriented

On the other side, less-productive employees are . . .

- Never satisfied with the job, company, or pay
- Always want to change the rules to suit themselves or they are political
- Get by with the minimum and never volunteer
- Offer "acceptable" feedback instead of real comments
- Have one foot out the door and are always looking for a better deal
- Reactive

Again, a simple truth explains it all: do unto others as you would have them do unto you.

> "Increasingly, the producing human being is a knowledge worker. Workers, as they did before the Industrial Revolution, own the means of production. The means is between their ears. They can take it with them whenever they leave and increasingly workers know that, and therefore have mobility. They are, in fact, not employees but paid volunteers. This implies a totally new social organization."
>
> —Peter F. Drucker, management guru

Nurse

9) Treat each employee as an appreciating asset.

New World Library is an example of a company with real values, and strong internal and external Customer Service programs. Marc Allen, the owner, believes in sharing, as described in one of his books. He splits profits with employees 50/50! When I last checked, the company had about ten employees and $15 million in sales. Its sales per employee are among the highest in the country—higher than Microsoft. And its profit margins mean employees share hundreds of thousands of dollars every year. You can bet that employees work with each other to serve Customers better. And New World Library's workforce is extremely stable, which makes maintaining good relationships with Customers, suppliers, authors, and other constituencies easier.

Network

10) Recognize employees have practical power.

Employees don't have to go the extra mile. They don't have to interact with others in a supportive fashion. Employees understand what minimum performance is expected and they determine, on their own, how much more to give.

Newsworthy

11) If you truly want to get the most from your employees, you must "enlist" them.

Enlist your employees every day by educating, marketing, and publicizing that your company is worthy of their efforts. When your company does something above the norm, let everyone know.

According to Jim:
Don't fear change. Embrace it enthusiastically. Encourage and drive it.

Natural

12) The steps necessary to create a strong internal Service culture are the same general steps necessary to create any organizational change.

A sustained effort from the top must recruit employees to make the necessary efforts to implement a new "culture." The following steps can help you to increase your internal Customer Satisfaction:

- Stay in contact with your Customers regularly.
- Show your Customers you are the consummate professional with extensive product knowledge.
- Find a way to make your Customers start "thinking" about your Services.
- Sell your Customers on ideas (rather than just products) by sharing proven case histories with them.
- Make your Customers' research for a resource an enjoyable experience.
- Make each one of your Customers know they are the most important Customer you have!

Navigate

13) Communicate a clear vision and specific goals.

Every change program must have a clear vision and specific goals that are repeatedly communicated to employees. Focusing on external Customer Service is an excellent key to change. Employees understand its importance. When an organization is in crisis, it can usually be saved by more Customer business. Even in nonprofit organizations, employees can easily see that if Customers aren't happy, their jobs won't be secure.

Internal Customer Service is also a message employees will resonate to because it's for them. Most companies try to motivate change to be more efficient. This not only has little personal appeal for employees, it also often threatens them. By pairing internal and external Service, you have a strong message employees can buy into.

"Do ordinary things with extraordinary love."
—Mother Teresa

Near

14) Involve all employees.

By obtaining the input of employees early, you not only get ideas, you also reduce resistance to change. When employees are involved in creating the program, they're more committed to carrying out the program.

Narrate

15) Repeat your message.

The more employees understand their importance within the organization and their personal contributions to make the workplace more productive, the better your chance of increasing the cooperative interaction of each coworker.

Resisting something you don't understand is natural. Repetition of an internal Service message helps reduce the resistance, which leads to a more cohesive effort to achieve established goals.

Negotiate

16) Ask coworkers to resolve their problems themselves.

If you're trying to build a bridge among coworkers, allow them to fix any problems that arise immediately. The interaction can create a better understanding of procedures and policies, which can foster a team effort. The best relationships of coworkers are personalized. Empower employees. Treat them like adults. Tell them they are the caretakers of the company.

> "Moses, racing his harassed people across the desert, came to the Red Sea and, snapping his fingers, called, 'Manny!' Up, breathless, came Manny, the publicity man. 'Yes sir?' 'The boats!' 'What?' 'The boats,' said Moses. 'Where are the boats to get us across the Red Sea?' 'Oh, my God! Moses, with all the news items and human interest stories, I forgot!' 'You what?' 'I forgot.' 'You forgot the boats?' cried Moses. 'The Egyptians will be here any minute! What do you expect me to do—talk to God, ask him to part the waters, let all of us Jews across, and drown the pursuing Egyptians? Is that what you think?' 'Boss,' said Manny, 'You do that and I'll get you two pages in the Old Testament!'"
>
> —Leo C. Rosten, *The Joys of Yiddish*

Net

17) Create clear rewards.

What are you doing to focus on the appreciation of your employees' work? People like to be recognized. They especially like to be recognized in front of their peers. Make recognition part of every program run by your company, no matter how small the actual prize.

New

18) Build excitement.

Make new programs fun. Games create excitement, so create a game with points where everyone can win. As the competition builds, it will eventually crest at the top. If you continue to maintain that crest, it can sustain a culture change that's more permanent. Games (or *gamification* as they're now called) have proven that our competitive nature can be used to great advantage if the programs are fun, relevant, and measurable.

Normalize

The final result of great internal Customer Service is the capability of your company to attract, keep, and satisfy long-term employees. Customers appreciate stability in the people they deal with, so this furthers organizational success. This, in turn, makes rewarding and keeping employees easier. To get started, create a program with clear rewards.

Newfound

In his book, T. Scott Gross says all labor is emotional labor. Gross reports that "a survey of managers estimated that motivated employees would be 30 percent more productive than those who were not motivated."

—T. Scott Gross, author of
Outrageous! Unforgettable Service . . . Guilt-Free Selling

This might be an underestimate.

Greg Steltenpohl, a founder of the fresh juice company, Odwalla, said the earlier owners tested procedures themselves to see how long they would take. By doing this, the owners thought they would know how many people should be hired to do the work. The owners were typically 70 percent more productive than the employees. Why? Because most employees aren't emotional about their workplace—they aren't emotionally connected to their jobs. A well-done incentive program can bring some of the employee emotional connection back to the workplace.

Nominate

19) A good incentive program sets up a series of rewards that employees can achieve for specific performances.

Traditionally, incentive programs have been most common for salespeople because their performance is easily measured. More recently, incentive programs are being increased for other employees as their contributions are being recognized. One of the strongest incentives is personal recognition. An incentive program formalizes personal recognition with clear rules, which enable people to achieve and be rewarded objectively.

Numerate

20) Create a program to reward the internal Customer Service within your organization. Here's how:

Review All the Available Information
- What did your company do in the past to educate employees and encourage them to work together?
- What do you know about the success or failure of the program?

- If you ran the same program today, would the results be different?
- Do you have any suggestions or complaints that would make a similar program run more smoothly?
- Would management support this effort?

Define the Role of the Employees
- Who are the participants?
- What are the limitations, if any, of the participants' abilities to solve problems?
- What is the dollar amount granted to the employees to solve a problem?

Set Measurable Objectives or Goals
- Realistic—how realistic is the objective?
- Measurable—how easy to understand is the measurement?
- Understandable—how easy was it for the coworkers to understand and agree to these objectives?

According to Jim:
The first sale any of us have to make is to ourselves. Commit 100 percent to the important shifts in your life.

There's a window of opportunity when Customer problems arise. Let me be clear. Customers are frequently annoyed, confused, lack the facts, don't articulate solutions clearly, and might have expectations that are neither implied nor promised. That said, the Customer is never wrong. Customers vote with their money. They now have a voice. They have a platform that is anchored to the Internet. The faster you can solve the problem, the better your changes are of keeping your Customer. The longer it takes to resolve the problem, the greater the perception that the problem escalates. Problems offer you the opportunity to make an impression on your Customer that exceeds the expectations of the performance of the product or Service. Even the most critical Customer knows that mechanical, technical, and personal tastes often influence outcomes. Within this center of confusion is when Customer Service can make or break the relationship.

First, let me define the *circle of confusion*. As a professional photographer, I learned that all light rays came through a lens and became reversed. Top was bottom, right was left, and so on. When the image was presented to film, it became negative. White was black, black was white. A negative, when printed, reversed that process again and the image was a representation of the original.

Second, that's the same with a complaint. Make the negative positive and your process will use the circle of confusion to produce brilliant images.

Your organization can recover from almost anything negative if the results can be made positive.

Creative Strategy
  I. What are you trying to accomplish overall?
  II. How does this integrate with the overall company objectives?
  III. How do you get there from here?

Review the Objectives and Strategies with Management
  I. Make sure you have a top management "champion" for the program.
  II. Be certain the support staff is involved.
  III. Make sure all department heads understand this program.
  IV. Be certain you can deliver good products and Services. (If the product is poorly made, tastes bad, or is overpriced, employees can't be proud of what they do.)

Determine Tactics
  I. Communications and promotion—How will this program be launched? How will it be communicated throughout its life?
  II. Administration—Who is in charge? What resources do you have to allocate?
  III. Training and research—Could anything short-circuit this program? How do you train your participants? Have you involved all departments? Did you research what the competition is doing?
  IV. Turnaround time—What is a reasonable time period to accomplish this goal?
  V. Accurate information—How will you deliver progress reports in a timely manner to participants?
  VI. Trust—How will you keep promises?

VII. Exceeding expectations—Can you deliver more than you promised?

Follow-Through

A properly executed plan sets the tone for continued internal Customer Service, just like the fighter pilot who has the enemy in sight gets a tone before he fires his missile. A *tone* is the signal to the pilot that he has the target lined up and ready for firing his missile. In your programs, you should get a smile, followed by a tone of joy, which alerts you that your employee is ready to accept your plan.

Remember, the program isn't successful until the winners say so. If they feel they're winners, the sponsoring company will also be a winner.

Track the Program

I. Assign responsibility.
Provide reports to each level: participants, lower-, and upper-management.
I. Fine-tune throughout your program.
II. Listen to your participants. Accept any new ideas and try to use them. Respond appropriately and in a timely manner.
III. Take what you hear seriously and act fast.
IV. Create a new program built on the success of the recently completed one.

Put Nurturing into Action

- Gather input from all employees about how they see current internal Customer Service. (In organizational climate studies, you might measure cooperation, support, morale, job satisfaction, and so forth.)
- Ask employees what they want from their jobs.
- Calculate your turnover and absenteeism rates, and what they cost you.
- Include costs of "dropping the ball" for Customers.
- Make sure top execs regularly spend time on the front line.
- Find ways to turn your organizational pyramid upside down to emphasize Customers and to support your staff.
- Develop a clear message about internal Customer Service and disseminate it throughout your organization.
- Develop recognition programs where employees can acknowledge each other for internal Service.

- Develop a larger incentive program where all employees can earn bigger rewards for internal Service.
- When employees are treated as Customers, they take care of your Customers.
- Unrivaled investing in internal Customers results in exceeding external Customer expectations.

Action Summary

1. A dissatisfied employee won't provide exceptional Customer Service on a long-term basis.
2. Internal Customer Satisfaction is directly related to external Customer Satisfaction, profits, and growth.
3. Internal Customer dissatisfaction leads to external Customer dissatisfaction and loss of profits.
4. Internal Customer Satisfaction is the key element in creating and keeping long-term Customers.

Your opportunity for business success has never been more plentiful. Harness the power of your team to dominate your marketplace. The results will be most gratifying!

Remember, D A T I N G Is Fun!

According to Jim:
Keep negatives out. Your positive attitude rubs off on others, creating a more harmonious environment for your Customers.

James Feldman

19 Meaningful Ways to Nurture Your Internal Customers

1. Internal Customers are your coworkers.
2. Coworkers must interact before they can act on the behalf of a Customer.
3. A good internal Customer care program can be achieved by education.
4. Employees must work together to form a cohesive unit that can Service the Customers of a business.
5. "Yes" must replace "No." "Can do" must replace "It's not my job."
6. A people-approach to business results in profits.
7. Retain existing employees and encourage them to return to work each day. (Happier employees also save you money and perpetuate a positive culture by recruiting new applicants with similar attitudes and expectations.)
8. Increase each employee's awareness of their need to exceed coworker expectations.
9. Increase the commitment of each person to be responsible for coworker Satisfaction. Revise policies and procedures whenever necessary to increase overall satisfaction.
10. Empower each employee with information and decision-making authority.
    - Make the workplace a positive place.
    - You can't exceed the expectations of your Customers unless you first exceed them for your employees.
    - Treat each employee as an appreciating asset.
    - Recognize employees have practical power.
    - If you truly want to get the most from your employees, you must "enlist" them.
11. Create a strong internal Service culture with the same general steps that are necessary to create any organizational change.
12. Communicate a clear vision and specific goals.
13. Involve all employees.
14. Repeat your message.

15. Ask coworkers to resolve their problems themselves.
16. Create clear rewards.
17. Build excitement.
18. Set up a good incentive program with a series of rewards that employees can achieve for specific performances.
19. Create a program to reward internal Customer Service within your organization.

New Management Principles are self-reinforcing and interlocking

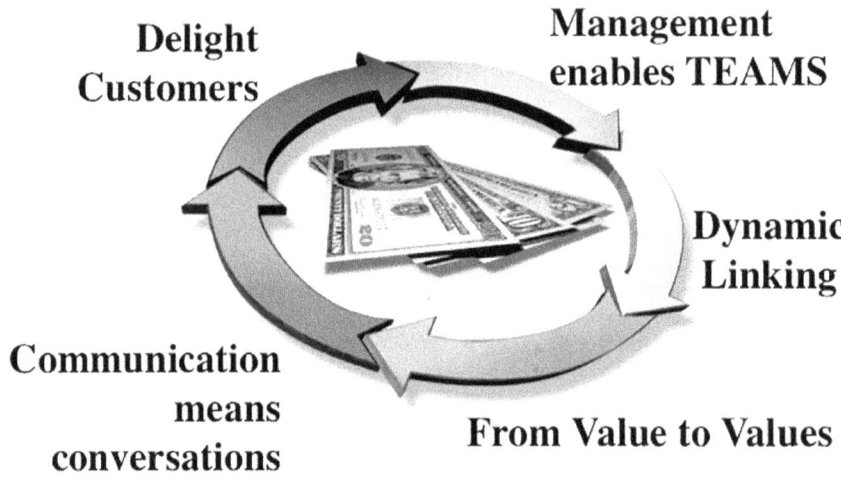

- Delight Customers
- Management enables TEAMS
- Dynamic Linking
- From Value to Values
- Communication means conversations

ATTITUDE is everything.
67% of all Customers leave because of a poor attitude, or indifference from company employee.

G Is for Guarantee

15 Ways to Guarantee Both Your Employees and Your Customers Are Satisfied

Guarantee

1) Guarantee that both your internal and external Customers are satisfied by showing them gratitude.

Go out of your way to guarantee that your internal Customers—your employees—are satisfied. If not, how can they satisfy your external Customers? Gratitude means rewarding them through incentives and promotions, and treating them just as you would like to be treated. If you do this, you'll keep them coming back for more.

> "Concentration is the secret of strength . . . in all management of human affairs."
> —Ralph Waldo Emerson

Gainful

2) To gain more Customers and build your business, first concentrate on the Customers you already have.

To alleviate stress, you need to stay focused on what you have that works—what you experience and what you enjoy—because the world is prepared to give you the message that you aren't doing enough. Customers are quick to tell you about your shortcomings and compare you to other organizations in which they received exceptional attention. To gain more business, first concentrate on the Customers you have already. Make them want to tell others about you and your Services. Offer them a reason to continue to do business with you; gain their trust, so they want to tell others. Deal with a Customer complaint fairly. If you aren't going to agree with your Customer, try to reason with them. Take the time to explain why you can't comply with their request. Remember, it costs 91 percent more to get a new Customer than to retain an older one (*Wall Street Journal* survey).

> "You gain strength, courage, and confidence by every experience in which you really stop to look fear in the face. You are able to say to yourself, 'I lived through this horror. I can take the next thing that comes along.' You must do the thing you think you cannot do."
>
> —Eleanor Roosevelt

Gesture

3) Your gestures will either convey thankfulness or indifference to your Customers.

The more you focus on gratitude, the more you can diminish stress and open the doors to bring greater things in to your life. When you focus on and think about good things, you become a better person. If you spend a good portion of your day remembering the delicious lunch you had, the kind words someone said to you, or the beautiful compliment you gave someone, you are focusing on gratitude, which can lead to a much less-stressful existence.

It's the same with having a Customer. No matter what your Customer says, try to be grateful they are still your Customer. Sometimes a Customer stretches the limits of your tolerance. At other times, a Customer can stretch your sense of fair play. And, in some instances, this all seems just plain ridiculous. To express your gratefulness to your client for their business, make a gesture of good faith that keeps your Customer wanting more. Do something that says "Thank You . . . we appreciate your business." How about when you order a pound of meat at the deli and you're given a few extra ounces at no charge? What about getting the free refills of your soft drink? And how about free freight or a liberal returns policy? Do these seem like wasted gestures to you? Make your Customers enthusiastic about doing business with you.

> **"We act as though comfort and luxury were the chief requirements of life, when all that we need to make us happy is something to be enthusiastic about."**
>
> —Charles Kingsley

Garnish

4) Garnish your Customer Service with unexpected, pleasant extras to let your Customers know they're special to you.

Living with gratitude is probably one of the simplest and most effective ways to manage stress. Make it a point to pause on a daily basis and be thankful for what you have. As a lifestyle coach, I ask my clients to go through this exercise. I ask them to tell me what they did well in the last seven days to help them accomplish goals or what happened to make them grateful. I ask them to write this information down, to take notes, and to read the notes aloud to themselves. Taking the time to think about the positive things that have happened to you makes getting through the tougher times easier.

As a businessperson, I try to add something to the plate . . . to garnish it with something unexpected. A personal thank you note, a free gift, or something Customers didn't expect. A restaurant that places a flower on every table or offers a free appetizer to your meal makes you think, *Wow! That was great and such an unexpected treat. I think I'll eat here more often.* And, when you find yourself getting upset, remember the Customer who complains is really giving you an opportunity to fix something or offer a gesture of good will to keep them from leaving to find your competition.

> "Acting in anger is like putting to sea in a storm."
>
> —Benjamin Franklin

Gentle

5) Be gentle with yourself when you start new rituals; take baby steps.

Now, you might read this and think, *That makes a lot of sense,* but until you practice being thankful, it won't work. You might need to get into a daily ritual. Every day when you get out of bed, hesitate for a moment and be thankful for what occurred the day before. It can put you in the right mindset. Rituals on a daily basis can decrease stress.

I suggest this because, if you apply it at home, you can take it to work. It's unlikely you'll use it at work, and then try to bring it home. So, be gentle with yourself. Start with something you *can* control . . . your life. Then, try to make it happen with your Customers, your associates, and so forth. This ritual is a process that takes time and energy. And baby steps make it possible. Let go of things that are out of your control. You'll endure much less stress and success is greater if you don't worry.

> "When angry, count to ten before taking action; when very angry, count to one hundred."
>
> —Thomas Jefferson

The things you often don't discuss, things that bother or worry you, can grow and fester. The more you suppress those things you don't want to admit, the deeper and bigger those problems become. For example, in the beginning of a business or dating relationship, you might act a certain way because you want the other person to like you. You want to continue to see that person, so you conceal the fact that what you're doing isn't really in sync with who you are. Or, you try to ignore a habit the person has that bothers you. You don't want to bring those feelings to the surface—to express them to yourself or anyone else—and the more you push down those feelings, the more stress they create in your life.

Whether it's a date or a business relationship, at some point, these feelings have to surface.

When I first started my business, I didn't want to offend any Customer, even if we discussed issues on which we weren't in total agreement. Over the years, I dropped that facade. If I say something someone else doesn't agree with, I know that's fine. I'm not here to have everyone love me—that's a tough place for most of us to reach. I do try to reason with my Customers, but the bottom line comes down to my own personal belief system. Sometimes I have to remove myself from a discussion and turn it over to someone else to handle. I empower the other person to make the decision, knowing I simply can't do it.

Another example is the person who hasn't learned how to say "No." They agree with things all the time because they're asked. They continue to pick up the neighbor's kids every time they're asked, and they say "Yes" to every family function. But this person is suppressing true feelings. If you continue to say "Yes," even if you're exhausted, it's eventually going to tear you down.

This creates a lot of stress. Apply that same policy to your business.

Is keeping this particular Customer important, when you know every time they call it's going to be another issue? Sometimes you simply have to let go.

> **"We must select the illusion which appeals to our temperament and embrace it with passion, if we want to be happy."**
>
> —Cyril Connolly

Gaze

6) Look around for ways you can serve the greater good of others.

To continue on the path of gratitude, you need to look outside yourself. While it's easier to stay focused on yourself, that can cause more stress in your life. Start to look at serving others. This can be as simple as allowing a car to pull ahead of you in traffic or acknowledging someone who gave you a break. Serving is all about giving. It could be giving a smile or a little of your time. A "simplicity movement" is happening in this country, and part of it is going back to how people used to act in the early 1900s. For example, if a neighbor's car broke down, half the neighborhood would try to help him fix it. I still marvel that, in the South, cars pull over to let a funeral pass. Observers still take off their hats and sunglasses in respect. I hope we haven't lost the simple courtesies that make us human beings. Look around you and observe. You see it happen and you don't process it. A man opens a car door or stands up for a woman when she enters the room. Someone sends a handwritten thank you note or a note of condolence. You can see it if you want to . . . look around you and take notes . . . it's out there for you to find, observe, and emulate.

> **"The first law of success in this day, when so many things are clamoring for attention, is concentration—to bend all energies to one point, and go directly to that point, looking neither to the right nor to the left."**
>
> —William Matthews

Give

7) Find continuous ways to give to others around you, including your clients.

I read a story about a dog who recently had puppies, and about four of those pups had serious health problems. The veterinarian found three other vets in the area and they all took a puppy home, so they could give it the care it needed. They did it as a way to serve humanity, and they did it without charging a fee. Their mutual reaction was simply a way to give more of themselves.

What have you done to make your Customers want to do business with you? How can you convey that you really care without being a soft touch to every simple complaint or Customer knee-jerk reaction?

> **"When love and skill work together, expect a masterpiece."**
>
> —John Ruskin

Gratis

8) Expect nothing in return when you give.

Giving of yourself automatically decreases the stress in your life because you're outside your own head and making a difference in the world around you. It's the care mentality. You're getting so much back by feeling connected to the human spirit. If we could all do that and feel more connected—even in little ways—I believe stress would be decreased in our lives. Give time. Give a hug. Give a warm handshake. Thank your Customer for giving you their business.

Ask your Customer what you can do to make their experience more pleasant. Ask about what you can do to introduce yourself to others through your Customer. Ask for a referral. If you give, you get back. Give as often as you can. Give to others without thinking; they'll give back and you might be surprised.

> "There are risks and costs to a program of action, but they are far less than the long-range risks and costs of comfortable inaction."
>
> —John F. Kennedy

Goodwill

9) Create good will whenever you can. This kind of care is free but, to Customers, it's invaluable.

We recently received some returned merchandise. The return address said C&J, P.O. BOX xxxx, LA. Nothing was inside except a totally broken item. No warranty. No bill of sale. Nothing else. We knew the Customer would be calling in a few weeks to complain because we didn't respond, but we couldn't. Or could we? I suggested we drop a postcard in the mail to the address with a note saying,"We are in receipt of your returned merchandise. Please contact us at our toll-free number."

I also suggested we send the postcard out three times, four days apart. Then, we could document to the Customer that we had done everything possible to reach them. Once they called us, we could get their name, find the date of purchase, and decide how to handle the problem.

> "All business proceeds on beliefs and judgments of probabilities, not on certainties."
> —Charles W. Eliot

Until we had the proper information, though, we could either sit and wait for that inevitable irate phone call, email, or letter, or become proactive and try to find the information.

> "The greater the obstacle, the more glory in overcoming it."
> —Molière

Generate

10) Generate a list of ways in which you can make it easy for your Customer to do business with you.

You must be consciously aware in life to start thinking about feeling gratitude for what you have. As people, we can't continue only to be concerned about our own lives, our own responsibilities, and ourselves.

A world out there needs our help. Customers want to do business with people who want to serve them. And they want to avoid those who are selfish, self-centered, and self-serving. Yet, how many companies make it so difficult to do business with them that you wish you had other choices?

Cable television? Car rental companies? Certain airlines? Some companies seem to go out of their way to make it difficult to conduct business, while others make doing business a pleasure. Find companies you like doing business with and ask yourself, "What makes me want to do business with this firm instead of that other one?" Generate a list of ideas and concepts you can apply to your own business.

The Golden Rule applies to Customers. Treat them exactly as you want to be treated when you are someone else's Customer.

"Genius is eternal patience."
—Leonardo da Vinci

Guest

11) Treat your Customers the same way you would treat a welcomed guest in your home.

As a child, whenever my family would move to a new house, three or four neighbors would arrive with food, introduce themselves, and offer to help just as soon as the moving van pulled away. But I can't tell you how many times I've heard of people moving into a neighborhood and living there for six months or longer without ever meeting any of their neighbors. I think we've lost something when we forget how important it is to go over to a new neighbor and say "Hello." This goes back to living consciously, to being aware, to deciding when you wake up each day that you're going to look for ways to serve others. And, just in case you forget, your Customers will remind you. Remember, Customers who have a choice are going to exercise that choice. They'll use it to remind you they can do business elsewhere. Treat your Customer as you would treat a guest in your home. They come over to be served and hosted. They don't expect to be charged to make a local phone call, to use the bathroom, or even for a drink refill. If your business Customer were treated as you treat a welcome guest in your home, would you be doing something different? If your answer is "Yes," then change the policies and procedures to mirror your home rules.

"Don't go around saying the world owes you a living. The world owes you nothing; it was here first."
—Mark Twain

Get-Rid-of-It

12) Clear your work areas of clutter and you'll ultimately clear your mind as well.

When you unclutter your life, you unclutter your mind. As an experiment, pick a specific room in your home. If you get rid of everything in that room except the bare essentials, your mind might become more relaxed.

For example, I've walked into hotel suites where there's a table with only one plant on it, a nightstand with only a lamp and a clock radio, and a bathroom with an empty countertop, except for small bottles of shampoo and conditioner. I felt so relaxed. The room was totally uncluttered, the energy was flowing freely, and I didn't feel smothered. Proponents of the art of feng shui—the Chinese art of placement—believe when you go into an environment that's truly clear and clean, you have a greater ability to be creative, focused, and attentive.

> **"The shoemaker makes a good shoe because he makes nothing else."**
>
> —Ralph Waldo Emerson

Gush

13) Let your enthusiasm for your Customers' Satisfaction pour out in every detail of the Service you provide to them.

The more you look for ways to unclutter your life, the freer and more productive you feel. Although uncluttering goes beyond the physical sense of the word, the easiest way to begin is to unclutter physically.

Then, look at uncluttering your life from a human perspective. What people in your life have you moved past? What people have you had as friends for years and years, even though they haven't supported your growth? The more you look for ways to unclutter every aspect of your life, the less stressed you'll be. Now apply all this to your Customers. Graciously welcome them.

Be grateful your Customers exist. And make them feel like a much-wanted guest, instead of an unwanted intruder. Give attention to detail and provide meaningful information. Take personal responsibility to assure your Customers the Services offered are, in fact, supplied. Make your Customers grateful they chose to do business with you and ask them to tell their friends if they're satisfied.

> **"My idea of an agreeable person is a person who agrees with me."**
>
> —Benjamin Disraeli

Apparently, most Customers have also heard this expression.

Gifts

14) Offer gifts, which don't cost you a cent, that you can give back.
- *The Gift of Listening* . . . but you must REALLY listen. No interrupting, no daydreaming, no planning your response. Just listen.
- *The Gift of Affection* . . . be GENEROUS with appropriate hugs, kisses, pats on the back, and handholds. Let these small actions demonstrate the love you have for family, friends, and contributors.
- *The Gift of Laughter* . . . clip cartoons, and share articles and funny stories. Your gift will say, "I love to laugh with you." Do this often.
- *The Gift of a Compliment* . . . A simple and sincere, "You look great in red," "You did a super job," or "That was a wonderful meal" can make someone's day.
- *The Gift of a Favor* . . . Every day, go out of your way to do something kind. Do it without regard for payback. Do it because you want to, not because you feel you should.

- *The Gift of a Cheerful Disposition* . . . The easiest way to feel good is to extend a kind word to someone. Really, it's not that hard to say, "Hello" or "Thank you."
- *The Gift of a Handwritten Note* . . . This can be a simple "Thanks for the help" note or a full sonnet. A brief, handwritten note could be remembered for a lifetime and might even change a life. Tell your contributor you care.
- *The Gift of Solitude* . . . At times, we want nothing more than to be left alone. Be sensitive to those times and give the gift of solitude to others. They might not give it to you, but you can always give it to them.

Give Back

15) Give back to others. Everyone of us is obligated to someone. First, to our fellow work associates. They really protect us. We're on the same T•E•A•M.

We need each other. First, be the kind of associate others want to work with.

Be kind, be generous, and be grateful.

Second, be generous to your suppliers. They are the backbone of your company. Without suppliers, you have nothing to sell. There wouldn't be any company functions without suppliers. You can't act alone. Remember, suppliers can be the major resource for new business. They interact with others who may be potential Customers for what you offer.

Third, remember that Customers talk to other Customers. Either they convince others to do business with your firm if their experience was good or to avoid your company if their experience was bad. Customers are the reason we're all in business. I don't believe that Customers are always right, but there's no reason to tell them so unless you no longer want them as Customers.

James Feldman

According to Jim:

To further guaranteed success:
   Follow successful organizations.
   Hang out with successful people.
   Learn from the best, so you can get better.

DATING your Customer

Dazzle

Anticipate

Treat

Innovate

Nurture

Guarantee

Action Summary

Simple ideas can sometimes be the catalyst that raises your company above the competition.

1. Simple thank-you gestures go a long way. This is nothing new or foreign. Your mother always told you to be grateful and to express your gratitude.

2. Spread the word. No matter how you do it, tell others so they tell others, and so on. The simplest way is to write a note and show your Customers how grateful you are that they did business with you. Express your understanding that you know they have a choice and, when they do business with you, they continue to exercise that choice.

3. Make your advisors your business. Ask your advisors for their advice. Encourage them to interact with you. In a sense, this is a sign you care about your advisors' opinions and they'll normally be flattered. Just like when you're on a date, ask your date what they liked or didn't like. It's amazing to find out what your date appreciated most was just that you cared enough to ask what they thought.

4. Reward new Customer business by upping the ante. Salespeople who bring in new business should get a higher commission than returning business.

5. After the Customers have been with the company and made multiple purchases, encourage your sales force to go after new business by requesting a referral from your existing Customers. Be grateful to the Customer by offering some form of incentive or VIP treatment. Together, repeat Customers and incentivized employees can keep your existing base, while increasing your number of Customers.

6. Go to the center of gravity . . . where the business meets the Customers. Ask both your employees and Customers to participate. Lexus dealers offer a free breakfast once a month. For the price of pancakes or eggs, participating dealers get invaluable results.

7. Invite both your employees and Customers to sit in on focus groups or other interactive events. Use them to test new products, or to react to policy or pricing changes. Recognize your Customers with some form of tangible, viewable certificate, pin, mug, plaque, or something they can use to "brag" to others.

8. Reread the chapter on innovation. Any new idea that shows your Customers and employees you're grateful will come back to your business in terms of longevity.
9. Review the previously listed gifts, which don't cost you a cent.
10. Success often hinges on simplicity, creativity, and warmth. Be grateful to both your Customers and your employees. Without either, you have no business.

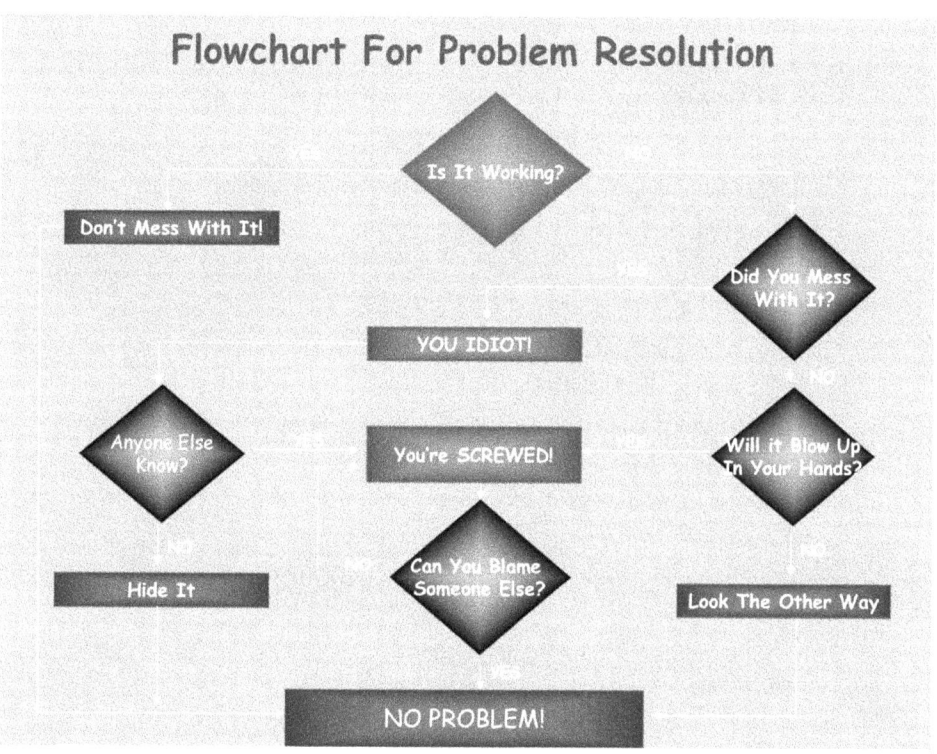

14 Guidelines to Customer Service Excellence

1. Be grateful for all your blessings and spend time with those who are special to you.
2. To gain more Customers and build your business, first concentrate on the Customers you already have.
3. Your gestures will either convey thankfulness or indifference to your Customers.
4. Garnish your Customer care with unexpected, pleasant extras to let your Customers know they're special to you.
5. Be gentle with yourself when you start new rituals. Take baby steps.
6. Look around for ways you can serve the greater good of others.
7. Find continuous ways to give to others around you, including your Customers.
8. Expect nothing in return when you give.
9. Create good will whenever you can. This care is free for you but, to Customers, it's invaluable.
10. Generate a list of ways in which you can make doing business with you easy for your Customer.
11. Treat your Customers the same way you would treat welcomed guests in your home.
12. Clear your work areas of clutter and you'll ultimately clear your mind as well.
13. Let your enthusiasm for your Customers' Satisfaction pour out in every detail of the Service you provide to them.
14. Offer gifts, which don't cost you a cent, that you can give back.

When you don't use a systematic process, you'll find it's difficult to pinpoint where breakdowns occur. More importantly, when you're successful, you'll find it difficult to repeat what you did that made the transaction go well.

THE COMPLAINT MANAGEMENT MODEL
PROBLEM RESOLUTION

STAGES OF INQUIRY	I DISCOVERY	II CONFIRMATION	III RESOLUTION
Customer Behavior	Inquiry Request Question Complaint	Acknowledgment	Acceptance
Employee Objectives	1. Establish relationship 2. Suspend own values 3. Further inquiry 4. Maintain composure	1. Isolate critical issue(s) (situation, problem, transaction) 2. Represent business	1. Develop plan of action 2. Gain commitment
Employee Responsibility	1. Attend 2 Listen 3. Respond	1. Attend 2. Listen 3. Respond 4. Identify 5. Clarify	1. Attend, listen, respond 2. Select strategy 3. Negotiate agreement action
Primary Skill	1. Empathic Listening	1. Appraisal Problem-solving	1. Negotiation 2. Decision-making
Outcome	1. Relationship established 2. Interchangeable exchange	1. Critical issue(s) identified 2. Solution(s) generated	1. Issue resolved 2. Follow-up

According to Jim:

Life is about solutions, connections, and leverage. Ask What? So What? Now What? Create a roadmap for how to manage shifts.

What happens when you've tried to satisfy an unhappy Customer and nothing seems to work? You must keep on trying. If you don't, this can result in a very unhappy Customer. This Customer will go on the Internet, file complaints, and tell everyone about how unhappy they are with your company.

The percentage of Customers who simply won't return to do business is between 30 and 50 percent. That's bad enough, but they want others to know about it. They make it a priority to warn others not to patronize your business. Wouldn't it be equally fair that, if they were happy, they would tell others? Nope. That's what you get paid for . . . to satisfy your Customers. Yet, if you exceed their expectations, they *will* tell others, which is the goal of every organization. Word-of-mouth is now the most powerful marketing tool available to any business. Using social media, blogs, articles, and other "public" soapboxes, consumers have found a voice.

So what does it take to satisfy an unsatisfied Customer?
Respond and do it quickly.

According to Jim:
*Remember, the Customer is always right—
no matter how wrong you think they are!*

6 Techniques for Handling A Challenging Customer

1. Establish a Common Ground
2. Listen and Show Concern
3. Use Appropriate Humor
4. Keep a Positive Attitude
5. Treat Customers like family or someone you really like
6. Cultivate Relationships

AHAs

D-A-T-I-N-G Your Customers® is about how you DAZZLE your Customers and build relationships.

D-A-T-I-N-G Your Customers® is all about ATTITUDE, which determines your altitude. Listen more than you talk. ACT delighted.

D-A-T-I-N-G Your Customers® is about how you TREAT each Customer uniquely. Fit their needs to a T.

D-A-T-I-N-G Your Customers® is about how you INNOVATE to solve problems better. It's about solutions for your Customers.

D-A-T-I-N-G Your Customers® is about how you NURTURE your employees, so they take better care of your Customers.

D-A-T-I-N-G Your Customers® has one objective: to GUARANTEE you continue to have Customers in the future.

Customer Care is just like D-A-T-I-N-G. The objective of both is to get the second date.

The Customer is still King and they know it. Think of the main task as bringing the Customer back.

What doesn't make sense is investing to attract new Customers, and then failing to match that effort with follow through.

It's called a Customer Return Policy. Don't wow them with long-term benefits to bring them back.

Being your own Customer on a regular basis is something you must do to become Customer-driven.

The market place looks totally different from where the Customer is standing. Make all decisions from their perspective.

The first temptation is to run the company to suit yourself, not your Customers. Suit your Customers or they'll suit themselves.

Reactions to what you communicate to your Customers is very difficult to forecast.

Your Customers aren't concerned with yesterday. What you did for them today is what really matters.

You don't know everything. You can't forecast reactions. Narrow your gaps in knowledge, instead of widening it.

Customer-driven means direct personal contact with the Customers who generate your business. Stay in touch. Often.

The most important skill to become Customer-driven is to listen.

It's not creative unless it sells. It must completely solve the problem without many resources or negative effects.

The "feel" of your marketplace isn't something you get second-hand.

Complaints can help you recover lost ground and improve your relationship with your Customer.

It isn't good enough to have 95 percent satisfied Customers. Five dissatisfied Customers tell twenty people. Satisfied Customers only tell one person.

Customers may not always be RIGHT, but there's no percentage in telling the Customer they're wrong.

Do Not Pass The Buck. Accept responsibility immediately, so your Customer complains only once.

If your Customer has a problem, you have a problem. Try to settle the complaint quickly.

Thank your Customer for complaining. Turn a complaint into a positive experience for both of you.

The "center of gravity" of your business should be as close as possible to the point where the business meets its Customers.

Don't let the accountants win. Sometimes it can cost less to serve the Customer better than to find new Customers.

Seeing your Customers, Suppliers, and Employees as people is what Customer-Driven is all about.

Imagine everyone has a sign around their neck that reads WIIFM (What's in it for me?). Make everyone feel important.

It costs more to get Customers than to keep them. Attracting new Customers costs 91 percent more than retaining an existing Customer.

Quality is the ultimate marketing weapon. Customer Satisfaction increases sales and profit margins. Keep your Customers happy.

When faced with a business decision, ask yourself, "What will this do to help bring the Customer back?"

The problem is to learn how to define the end results we want, and then to create the policies to achieve them.

The challenge for Customer Satisfaction is to provide more with less resources for Customers who demand more for less money.

Organizations need to heighten the awareness of the tremendous need for dedication to Customer Satisfaction.

Organizations should empower their employees to solve Customer complaints quickly without the need for a supervisor's approval.

A quality product is required, but quality alone won't retain your Customers or bring in new ones.

You must provide a quality product or Service at a competitive price, but that only makes you even with everyone else.

The highest expectation of Customers is to be treated like royalty. If you don't do this, Customers can find someone who will.

A very small percentage of your Customers take the time to complain. Most just quietly go away.

A Customer satisfied with your complaint resolution is going to tell at least five people about their experience.

A satisfied employee creates and keeps satisfied Customers. A dissatisfied employee can cost you Customers.

Quality products + Competitive prices × (Satisfied, trained employees) × (Efficient systems) = Customer-driven organizations.

Customer-driven organizations have the ability to attract, keep, and shift Customers to long-term relationships.

Stretch your goals by stepping out of your comfort zone if you want to make Shift Happen.

It's always up to you to make the first move. Customers expect you to offer tangible ways to keep them satisfied.

3 Ps make my decisions. P = Pleasure (Happy?) P = Profit (Save or make money?) P = Payback (I Owe Me? I Owe Them?) 2/3's minimum.

Strive for perfection or else. If 99 percent is good enough, then 2 million documents will be lost by the IRS.

Strive for perfection or else. If 99 percent is good enough, then in an hour, 22,000 checks will be deducted from the wrong account.

Strive for perfection or else. If you think 99 percent is good enough, two plane landings daily at O'Hare will be unsafe.

Strive for perfection. If 99 percent is good enough, then 18,322 pieces of mail will be mishandled by the post office.

Never say "I Don't Know." Instead, say, "That's good question. I'll check and find out for you."

Never say, "We can't do that!" Instead, say, "Let's see what we can do for you." Irate Customers want to vent. Don't interrupt them.

Never say, "No." Instead, say, "We aren't able to do what you requested, but we can offer you this instead."

Never say, "You have to. . . ." The only thing certain is death and taxes. The rest is something we can work on.

A Customer is a human being with feelings and money to spend with you. A consumer is a statistic. Know the difference.

Be nonjudgmental. Celebrate diversity. Have an open mind. Listen with your eyes. Discover a win/win solution.

The Resolution Process: Define the Problem—Gather Information—Offer Alternatives—Evaluate the Solution—Take Action—Reaffirm Acceptance.

Customers want authenticity. Share your thoughts. Cultivate transparency. Be open. Listen for feelings, not just facts.

Customer Service isn't a department. Everyone is responsible for keeping your Customers happy.

Customers are smart and informed. They have access to resources, product information, and prices. Treat your Customers with respect.

Attitude is everything. The percentage of all Customers who leave because of a poor attitude or indifference from a company employee is 67 percent.

Clearly define your Customer Mission by communicating it to all levels of your organization. Develop measurement systems.

Never say, "They didn't get back to me." Expecting someone to get back to you stops the action. Take the initiative.

Never say, "I thought someone else was taking care of that." Excuses indicate a roadblock to action.

When your Customer tells you what they want, give it to them. Debating the resolution will lose a Customer.

Everyone is a salesperson in some way. When you Service a Customer, you're selling them a return visit to your business.

Don't let what you think you know about your Customer's request prevent you from learning what you need to do to solve it.

You can't exceed the expectations of your Customers if you haven't first satisfied your employees.

You don't want satisfied Customers. You want loyal Customers. Satisfaction is the minimum requirement to stay in business.

It's simple math. Retaining 5 percent of your Customers can make a 75 percent difference in your profits and increase referrals.

Merely satisfied Customers aren't particularly loyal or profitable. Concentrate on lifetime value and repeat business.

Over 100 years ago, the founder of AT&T was asked, "What's your business?" He responded, "Our business is Service."

Henry Ford said it best: "If we are not Customer-driven, our cars won't be either." We are all in the Service business.

People don't buy products. They buy the product of the product. They buy solutions to their problems.

Only two valid business purposes exist: to create Customers and to innovate. Price isn't what brings them back.

Stew Leonard, a grocer in Danbury, CT, says, "Rule #1: The Customer is always right. Rule #2: If the Customer is wrong, read #1."

We've learned to gravitate to the least mediocre treatment we can find. The by-product of mediocrity is price sensitivity.

Regardless of the industry, with few exceptions, the creation of a Customer is a lost art. Despite this, sales are made.

Customers are the "center of gravity" of business activity. In the beginning, there was the Customer; at the end, is a sale.

Customers have come to expect immediacy. Instant gratification is really time-based. Customers want it now.

We are in a deep depression and deterioration in the way we treat our Customers. Create a WOW CUSTOMER RETURN POLICY.

Be Genuinely Helpful—Don't take anything personally—Don't make assumptions—Reinforce Values—Be Impeccable with your word.

To solve a complaint: Focus on Discovery—Reaffirm Your Discovery—Create a Joint Resolution.

Customer Rapport-Building Tips: Establish a Common Ground—Listen—Be Positive—Show Concern.

Customer Satisfaction isn't enough. Today, Customer Loyalty is all that matters. Satisfaction is the minimum criterion.

First, determine where you want to go. Then, create the path to get there. Be specific. Create the mindset of a winner.

Truly great Customer Service affects every individual, every process, and every level of every organization.

Thinking strategically about Customer Service pays off. Provide Customer Service worth celebrating.

You can't win an argument with a Customer. The Customer's perception is all that matters. You can't change it.

Customer Service is an opportunity to build Customer confidence and trust with an unlimited potential to create relationships.

Every Customer defines great Service differently. And, for each Customer, that's the correct definition.

Many organizations are besieged by incompetence and rampant indifference to the art of delivering great Customer Service.

Exceptional Customer Service is the best competitive differentiation in today's global marketplace.

Quality of a product or Service isn't what you put into it, but what the Customer gets out of it.

Competition demands you stay alert and in tune with your Customer. Shift Happens!® and we all have to deal with it.

Customers pay you to sweat all the details, so it's easy and pleasant for them to use your products and Services.

Act with integrity in your relationships. Be compassionate, friendly, loyal, and treat your Customers well.

All businesses exist to create, Service, and retain Customers while making a profit as they deliver exceptional Service.

Handling complaints is the most misunderstood, overlooked, and undervalued part of Customer Service.

Procrastination is the natural assassin of attitudes. Speed has the power of "Yes we can" because it's the top priority.

Everyone should always go the extra mile in encouraging thorough, complete, and effective communication.

Establish a common ground. Customers relate to those people who are most like themselves. Establish a common ground quickly.

Don't fear change. Embrace it enthusiastically. Encourage and drive it.

Listen and Show Concern. Your Customers always want to talk about their most favorite topic: themselves, their wants, or their needs.

Customers love to talk about themselves. Listen and offer compliments, when appropriate.

Listening involves so much more than simply not talking. It's a matter of understanding your client.

Use humor. Humor builds rapport and shows your softer side. Humor also eases tension and breaks down mental barriers.

Keep a positive attitude. When you're positive and upbeat, people naturally want to be around you and do business with you.

Keep negatives out. Your positive attitude rubs off on others. It creates a more harmonious environment for your Customers.

A crash course on Customer Service: The ten most important words are "I apologize for our mistake. Let me make it right."

Treat Customers like family. Your Customers want to know that you have their best interests at heart.

A crash course on Customer Service: The nine most important words are "Thank you for your business. Please come back again."

A crash course on Customer Service The eight most important words are "I'm not sure, but I will find out."

A crash course on Customer Service: The seven most important words are "What else can I do for you?"

A crash course on Customer Service: The six most important words are "What is most convenient for you?"

A crash course on Customer Service: The five most important words are "How may I serve you?"

A crash course on Customer Service: The four most important words are "How did we do?"

A crash course on Customer Service: The three most important words are "Glad you're here."

A crash course on Customer Service: The two most important words are "Thank you."

A crash course on Customer Service: The MOST important word is "Yes." The result: marketplace distinction and advocates.

Approach Customer Care the same way you approach a date. Nurture it with good habits and constant care.

Customers can create long-term relationships that can help you sell them on ideas (rather than just products).

When Customers tell others to do business with you because they are satisfied, you become a leader in your field.

A quality product begins with a commitment to prevent Customer Care issues before they develop.

When you misinterpret your Customer's needs, it can sabotage your ability to give the best care to your Customer.

Businesses are losing Customers every day because they aren't treating Customers the way they say they will.

Garnish your Customer Service with unexpected, pleasant extras to let your Customers know they're special to you.

To gain more Customers and build your business, first concentrate on the Customers you already have.

Your Customers always think they're right. Don't try to prove them wrong. This only annoys your Customers.

Changes in the company are driven from the bottom up, the front lines closest to the Customers and/or issues.

The companies that get into trouble are the ones that can't respond quickly enough and adapt to Customer challenges.

If you want to continue to stay ahead of your competition, you must continually change and keep them guessing.

Approach situations and challenges with an open mind. Be creative in your solutions and you create your own luck.

To rise above the competition, use adventure and creativity to be unconventional in your solutions.

Having effective, open, and honest communication is critical for building great Customer Service relationships.

Inside every employee is more potential than even the employee realizes. Help unleash it.

Great managers are servants/leaders removing obstacles and enabling direct reports to succeed. They serve those they lead.

The best teams are those that work with each other and also interact with each other outside the office.

You don't want satisfied Customers.

**Satisfaction
is the minimum requirement to stay in business.**

ONLY IF ALL ELSE FAILS...

*Here's what you can "think"
about a Customer
who you no longer care about.*

**Whatever you do, don't say this to your Customers.
But do give yourself permission to think it. It may
help you smile during tough decisions.**

This is only for your personal use. I don't suggest you say this to any Customer. I repeat: *do not say this to your Customer!* But it might help you get through your reasons to say goodbye to a Customer who simply can't be satisfied. It's like banging your head on the table. I don't recommend that either, but sometimes it helps clear your head.

- We're all refreshed and challenged by your unique point-of-view.
- I'm already visualizing the duct tape over your mouth.
- The fact that no one understands you doesn't mean you're a genius.
- I don't know what your problem is, but I'll bet it's hard to pronounce.
- Any connection between your reality and mine is purely coincidental.
- We have plenty of talent and vision. I just don't give a damn.
- I like you. You remind me of when I was young and stupid.
- What am I? Flypaper for freaks?
- It's a thankless job, but I've got a lot of karma to burn off.
- No, my powers can only be used for good.
- How about never? Is never good for you?
- You sound reasonable. Time to up my medication.
- I'll try being nicer if you'll try being smarter.
- At least I have a positive attitude about my destructive habits.
- You are validating my inherent mistrust of unreasonable Customers.

How do I learn more about D ಌ A ಌ T ಌ I ಌ N ಌ G Your Customer® and the other Shift Happens!® topics?

Please visit our website at www.shifthappens.com or contact us via phone or email. The D-A-T-I-N-G Your Customer® Series is available as a Keynote presentation. We also have other topics, such as 3DThinking, Creating a Culture of Innovation, The Journey to Bright Ideas, Why I Love The "F" Word, and Thriving on Change.

More According to Jim and Lessons are free on this website.

If you want to learn more about Shift Happens!® presentations, please visit our website or call: **312-527-9111.**

For a complimentary evaluation, fill out the form at:
www.shifthappens.coachesconsole.com

www.shifthappens.com

James Feldman
Shift Happens!®
505 N. Lake Shore Drive
Suite 6601
Chicago, IL 60611

(312) 527-9111
(312) 527-9113 fax

jfeldman@shifthappens.com

ANYTHING NOT MOVING FORWARD, IS MOVING BACKWARDS.

Acknowledgments

Thank you to the millions of companies that have Customers. Each of them has the unique ability to create a long-lasting relationship, but they often don't. So many individuals have contributed to the wealth of information contained in this book, I can't possibly thank them all.

To Michelle Hove, who has been my great advisor. She constantly kept me grounded on this project over the many revisions, frustrations, and constant Customer service failures and successes I discovered. Michelle tempered my frustration with large companies that outsource their "service" to more enlightened organizations that simply dazzled me with their commitment to exceed my highest expectations. Every day, Michelle has taught me the true meaning of **D-A-T-I-N-G** Your Customer®.

To my favorite editor, friend, and muse Marcia Baker, who helps me learn the rules that govern clear and concise editing. Candidly, I am terrible at that skill and, fortunately, she is a master craftsman. Marcia is an artist with words. She is my wordsmith, my advocate, and my coach. She is a master at her chosen avocation. Marcia gets it. When necessary, she reworks the text tirelessly and exceeds my expectations at every level. We have collaborated since 1979 and we'll continue to do so until she edits my eulogy, which, of course, I have already written. If you need an editor, Marcia can help you. Contact her at bakerink2010@gmail.com. Marcia **DAZZLES** me.

Life is all about relationships and I am so blessed to have these people in my life: my brother from another mother, Francisco "TJ" Tejeda, Principal, Talisman Group, Creator EZ Baccarat & Dragon 7/Panda 8; Joseph Sugarman, founder of BluBlocker sunglasses; Dr. Nido Qubein, president of High Point University; Harvey Mackay, author, speaker, and business expert; and Stephen J. Karoul, President and CEO Euro-Asia Consulting, LLC. They all shared their personal examples of their common-sense approach to **ANTICIPATE** the results of Customer-focused marketing. They reminded me that if you **TREAT** Customers poorly, it often creates a lack of confidence, trust, and satisfaction. Each of these business experts think about **INNOVATIVE** ways to **NURTURE** those Customer relationships to **GUARANTEE** success.

Many thanks to everyone.

James Feldman

Build Your Customer Relationships with these tools.

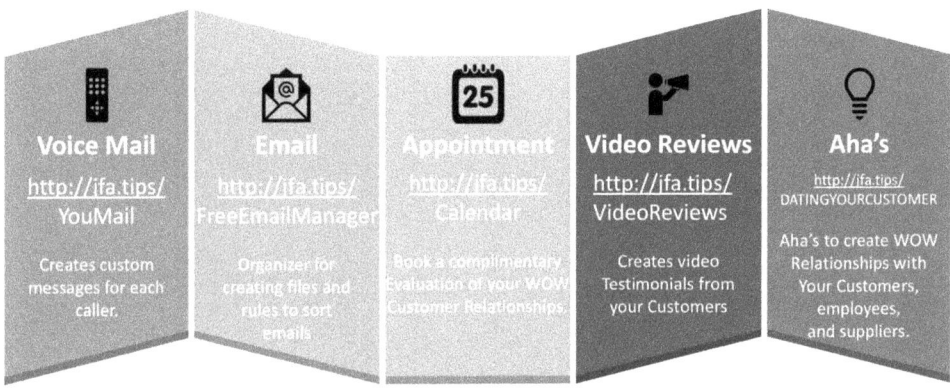

Voice Mail
http://jfa.tips/YouMail
Creates custom messages for each caller.

Email
http://jfa.tips/FreeEmailManager
Organizer for creating files and rules to sort emails

Appointment
http://jfa.tips/Calendar
Book a complimentary Evaluation of your WOW Customer Relationships.

Video Reviews
http://jfa.tips/VideoReviews
Creates video Testimonials from your Customers

Aha's
http://jfa.tips/DATINGYOURCUSTOMER
Aha's to create WOW Relationships with Your Customers, employees, and suppliers.

D⋅A⋅T⋅I⋅N⋅G
Your Customer

Encourage Customer passion for your organization by showing your passion for your Customers.

www.ingramcontent.com/pod-product-compliance
Lightning Source LLC
Chambersburg PA
CBHW081156020426
42333CB00020B/2522